CATASTROPHIC GUMBO

PART ONE:
THE SIGNATURE SERIES

Alvin JacQues

Order this book online at www.trafford.com
or email orders@trafford.com

Most Trafford titles are also available at major online book retailers.

Printed in the United States of America.

ISBN: 978-1-4269-6910-2 (sc)
ISBN: 978-1-4269-6911-9 (hc)
ISBN: 978-1-4269-6912-6 (e)

Library of Congress Control Number: 2011914606

Trafford rev. 10/21/2011

 www.trafford.com

North America & international
toll-free: 1 888 232 4444 (USA & Canada)
phone: 250 383 6864 ♦ fax: 812 355 4082

The Preface to

Catastrophic Gumbo

How did I get the name Catastrophic Gumbo because hurricane Katrina devastated various areas of Louisiana, Mississippi, Alabama and Florida with a multitude of occurrences all happening at the same time.

To me it was a super jumbo melting pot of Catastrophic Gumbo overflow throughout the Gulf South.

My name is Alvin JacQues, I'm the author of Catastrophic Gumbo and formally a Katrina survivor, I guarantee and trust my book will be one of the most dynamic group of stories ever experience.

This comprehensive book is filled with extraordinary drama, facts and details about the aftermaths of Katrina, you will experience a journey into science, history, geography and intensity from start to finish, and the level of truth will amaze you.

The insight and the scope of this powerful book will reveal the enormous amounts of devastation, causalities, and over all survival though thick and thin and beyond.

In August of 2010 was the fifth year anniversary of hurricane Katrina, I was televise on CBS, ABC, NBC, and CNN for having the most compelling group of true stories ever heard, and take my advice never underestimate the dynamics of a natural disaster like Hurricane Katrina, the legendary name Katrina was the pioneer into a new frontier inside America and throughout the world.

Various Aftermath stories
Inside Catastrophic Gumbo

And much more inside Catastrophic Gumbo
The list go's on and on

The Viewpoint of Global Hurricanes

A hurricane is Natures fury a single strike can coast billions every year, hurricanes claim Life's around the world, they are becoming more powerful, a hurricane is the worse. Weather phenomenon in the world

A hurricane is the devils brew of high wind surge, massive water surge, crashing waves and intense thunder storm it's an incredible blend of supernatural things happening all at once at the same time and lives depend on the outcome of the storm.

80 percent of hurricane form each year around the world, those that form inside the Atlantic ocean one third of them will reach America. 85 percent of the Atlantic hurricanes start in Africa,

The hot weather in Africa develops and promotes hurricanes, science calls this concept the Africa easterly wave system is when thunder storm cells reach between 23 to 39 miles per hour, it's then called a tropical depression.

28 tropical depressions develop every year inside the Atlantic ocean, But only 6 become hurricanes, these weather phenomenon's are fueled by thunder storms and warm water, at a temperature of 80 degrees which then increases the strength of tropical depressions to become bigger.

At 74 miles per hour the winds are then officially called a hurricane storm which can develop into the most destructive weather element of nature.

The Atlantic is the saltiest ocean in the world, salt helps the water to become heavier which gives hurricanes more punch power, the more salt the more punch.

The eye wall of a hurricane can reach up to 200 miles per hour the eye is the heart of the storm, here's five categories of wind speeds of hurricanes,

A category one is from 74 to 94 miles per hour
A category two is from 95 to 110 mph
A category three is from 111 to 130 mph
A category four is from 131 to 155 mph
A category five is from 156 to 200 mph
Very little now survive a category five it's to enormous.

Warm water and hot air temperature gives hurricane a boost kick to get bigger, a category four hurricane with a wind speed at 155 miles per hour can pick up and hold 2 billion tons of ocean water every 24 hours, which then gives the hurricane more power to have heavier storm surge and rain storms,

Hurricanes are the most dangerous entity of supernatural weather development on earth, they are very mysterious and unpredictable, the more water hurricanes pick up out of the ocean is the stronger the storm surge.

In august of 2005 Katrina's storm surge was your hundred miles wide in the gulf of Mexico she reach a category 5 but hit New Orleans between a category 3 and 4, Katrina was a mature jumbo hurricane that took hours to destroy New Orleans but will take years to rebuild.

Katrina was a blast of death because ain't no stopping a natural disaster in action until it's finish, the death of a hurricane gives scientist and experts more knowledge about the behavior patterns, In the last 20 years scientist and experts have gained more knowledge of hurricanes, but a mystery still remains what will hurricanes do with rising global temperatures around the world

It's likely the ocean water have heated up due to climate change, scientist and experts believe future hurricanes above maximum intensity of category 5 at 200 miles per hour, they believe future hurricanes will be at nearly 300 miles per hour which is the unthinkable and uncompromising to planet earth, and how will we survive that impact.

The Summary

In early august of 2005 Katrina was born off the coast lines of Africa then matured in the Atlantic ocean then she transferred to the gulf of Mexico, then she gained strength, above the water the surge was colossal, the waves in the water was between 25 to 40 feet high

Katrina was developing into a jumbo category 5 impact, the fuel of a hurricane in concert means the death warrant is written, in one day a hurricane can drop from a category 5 wind storm to a mild breeze.

But Katrina kept getting stronger in august 2005 because of the heated water in the gulf of Mexico with rising temperatures in the atmosphere on land it was a deadly combination to help increase her size and strength

The combination of heated water and hot air temperatures create more hurricanes per season, the power of a hurricane is awesome beyond comprehension.

The impact of a category 5 can create a domino effect of destruction on land, the winds surge can drop and pick up every 7 hours,

The second most dangerous part of a hurricane is the water surge, the stronger the wind surge means the stronger the water surge, the most deadliest part of a hurricane is water surge.

On August 29, 2005 Katrina brutally damage and destroyed much of New Orleans into the billions which then made Katrina one of the worse hurricanes storms ever to hit the city of New Orleans.

On August 29, 2005 other states was effected by Katrina which are Mississippi, Alabama, and Florida, they all had there own set of self explanatory problems to occur.

Before Katrina touch down on New Orleans, Mississippi, Alabama, and Florida many people was experiencing popping in their ears it's a sign from nature the pressures of a hurricane is near bye, it creates popping in the inner ears.

But the worse was yet to come, during the hit of the Katrina the levee was breaking due to heavy water surge, Once the Levees broke it put the city of New Orleans under 80 percent of water which is 250 billion gallons of water.

Many people was trap in tight with all odds against them, My neighborhood the historic CBD area had 18 feet of water, Meterie and St. Bernard parishes was reporting water level up to 27 feet high.

In the United States 80 percent of natural disaster are flood related,

Several weeks after Katrina out of the blue hurricane Rita came to New Orleans with heavy wind and water surge and reflood the city with several more feet of water for a second time, the city was then drowning in deeper water then before, New New Orleans is between 80 to 90 percent under water. Which was a harsh reality but very true reality.

The first set of stories you are about to read will take you on a compelling journey that will mesmerize you to grip your attention like never before, this book have detail of remarkable serious aftermaths featuring hurricane Katrina, the levee breach flood and New Orleans, the Superdome and many other stories you will find most interesting and compelling

These once in a lifetime true stories was witness and written by a respected Katrina survivor that is the author of this book series his name is Alvin Jacques he experience everything in New Orleans from start to finish he is capable of telling you everything you need to know step by step from experience on the scene.

Alvin Jacques lived inside the epicenter which was the most destroyed section of town in New Orleans, he is lucky to be alive, the information of these stories will take the readers into unforgettable journeys of dynamic situation and extraordinary measures of meticulous ordeals that happen by surprise due to hurricane Katrina in New Orleans..

The world could never forget hurricane Katrina and what she did to New Orleans, Mississippi, Alabama, and others, at that time billions of people were watching on global television the suffering and pains these ordeals created on August 29, 2005.

In the pass before Katrina came to New Orleans, the city would embrace hurricanes, because most storms would come and go with every little circumstances causalities or consequences, but Katrina was the big one that have change the perspectives of the people to be more concern of jumbo hurricane power,

Katrina was said to bring flooding of a Tsunami like proportion, which was a new thing to New Orleans, they will be caught off guard, trap and punish like never before which is the dramatics of these ordeal stories of Katrina and her aftermaths and what happen to the people without preparance or preparation.

This Story begins on August 26, 2005 which is three days before Katrina disfigure and dismantle New Orleans, Mississippi, Alabama and other surrounding area towns of the southern region coast lines.

On august 26, 2005 New Orleans only had voluntary evacuation in effect and the worse was yet to come, Katrina wind surge and water surge will be phenomenal of mega thrust proportion it will be nothing New Orleans has ever seen before, she will be the new kid on the block. Ready for action with compelling results. To change the outlook of hurricanes throughout the gulf south, hurricane Katrina was a unique theory of history, she was most original.

On august 27, 2005 100 thousand people in the city of New Orleans do not have any means of transportation, many of them don't have money for a bus, train, airplane or hotel most depend on welfare checks.

It's difficult for many to leave because New Orleans have a poverty rate of 23 percent which is more then twice the national average and the murder and incarceration rate is the highest level in the country of America.

The people of New Orleans honor hurricanes and many of the poorest people of New Orleans live in the ninth ward area which is between 3 to 6 feet below sea level

Before a hurricane hits the state will ask the federal Government to get involved that's were FEMA comes in Fema is home land security, Fema is to help plan a good strategy with the gross needs of the city and state to come up with a good plan of attack to help the citizens. Of the locations to be effected by the storm.

The director of Fema is Michiel Brown since 2003, Michiel Brown said to the media that Fema is not the organization it once was, after 911 Congress voted to downgrade Fema from a cabinet level agency to a homeland security department with a low budget.

Both Mississippi and Louisiana has declared a state of emergency which comes from the white house in Washington, On August 27, 2005 hurricane Katrina was a catastrophic category 3 she head straight for Louisiana and Mississippi and becoming a cataclysmic category 4 to 5 an is expanding rapidly

Moments later the shocking reality for the city of New Orleans is Katrina is now officially a monster cataclysmic level 5 headed for New Orleans in 3 different directions at the same time, the wind forces are from the north, east, and west, Katrina measurement from side to side is 400 miles in width & this storm is the big one

The extraordinary cataclysmic of Katrina is making it nearly impossible for anyone to leave surrounding areas without getting trap inside the dynamic velocity grip forces from various directions. Katrina stop all escapes out the cities. She was a force of nature. And full of surprises.

Inside New Orleans the 17th street canal is on the west side, the industrial canal is on the outside and the London avenue canal is in the gentilly area neighborhoods those levee canal walls were built in 1945 and was in need of update repairs and modifications in order to handle a storm surge of a category 3,4, or 5 hurricane. A storm surge is high winds pushing massive amount of water above normal sea level and much of New Orleans is between 4 to 6 feet below sea level this can cause catastrophic flooding at incredible heights

Max Mayfield is the director of the National Hurricane Center Max called the governor and mayor of New Orleans and told them of the enormity of Katrina's storm surge, Max was to the point, he said this hurricane is the big one and in my 32 years of being with the national hurricane center I've never seen a storm surge like Katrina.

Mayor Ray Nagen then told the city attorney he is ready to issue the first mandatory evacuation for the city of New Orleans, many people in the city are unaware of the ominous warning publicized on television and radio. And time was running out the hurricane was getting closer and closer.

On August 27, 2005 the nightclub bars and entertainment in the French quarter was rockin because the people of New Orleans honor hurricane every year.

On the other side of town the coast guards have helicopters and air planes on stand bye to be prepared, most of the oil companies in the gulf evacuated their oil rigs and the gulf accounts for 20 percent of the nations oil supply, and local and state officials are concern about our cities defense supports.

Saturday August 27, 2005 at 7:00pm Katrina is a category 5 cataclysmic hurricane hell bent on destruction rapidly increasing power from the gulf and carrying a awesome storm surge.

12 hours later on Sunday August 28, 2005 Katrina is 250 miles out in the gulf of Mexico, Katrina is now an extreme rare category 5 Cataclysmic monster forecast to come on shore in less then 24 hours she is now the most deadliest hurricane phenomenon in history and throughout the Atlantic ocean.

At 8:00am on August 28, 2005 the superdome begins taking in evacuees a mandatory evacuation was briefly mention but has not been put in active effect, it's only voluntary evacuation happening in New Orleans

The governor and mayor has the responsibility for getting people out of harms way, At 9:30 am August 28, 2005 President Bush called the governor of New Orleans to say he is concern about the people of New Orleans he would hope they would evacuate, at 10:00 am August 28, 2005 a mandatory evacuation is ordered, and was in effect 20 hours before Katrina touch shores of Louisiana.

The city of New Orleans has never seen a hurricane of this strength to hit it directly, the mayor then ordered and imposes a 6:00 p, curfew for everyone to get off the streets

The national weather center mention a apocalyptic warning which would seem suicidal to ignore most of the area will be uninhabitable for weeks or longer. Katrina was the biggest one on record.

One half of well constructed homes will have roof and wall failure all windows will blow out, air borne debris will be wide spread.

Persons, wildlife, pets and livestock expose to the wind force will face certain death if struck, but many are not leaving New Orleans it the home of the brave.

The police department has 1600 active police they cannot force people out of there own homes

For the people staying the police ask them to write there social security number on there bodies so when they find them they will know who you are so they don't have to finger print a decompose body.

The mayor dispatch buses to pick up residence at 12 locations to bring them to the superdome, the mayor wanted the people to come to the dome with there own supplies, like it was a camping trip.

The director of the national hurricane center which is Max Mayfield told the president the storm surge could push water over the top of the levee because Katrina is the big fat one.

In Mississippi governor Hayley Barbers stresses the seriousness of this situation to those that live alone the coast lines, they are at risk of a lot of causalities

In Louisiana State rep. Author Morrell an his wife Cynthia did not leave. And musician trumpeter Kermit Rufin left.

In the world of weather Katrina is the weapon of massive destruction, Katrina is a monster cataclysmic 5 which is the highest ranking hurricane from the Atlantic ocean.

A category level 5 hurricane with a wind speed of 175-200 miles per hour can pick up and hold over 2 billion tons of water from the gulf of Mexico every 24 hours, which then gives the hurricane more storm surge power, Katrina was the big one.

August 28, 2005

Katrina is a approximately 70 miles from the New Orleans shores the eye wall is 30 miles wide with a storm surge at 175 miles per hour, with a wind spread nearly 400 miles in width, Katrina is very big she's monster material, which is the most deadliest.

This storm surge is a once in a lifetime even the city of New Orleans has never seen a monster Jumbo hurricane of this strength to hit almost directly.

Mayor Ray Nagen has ordered people in the city to get out now every part of logic says go north, the national weather service says Katrina will cause enormous devastation damage across the gulf coast region.

Throughout the region residence prepare to face the storm, it's the day before the big show. Touchdown.

A system of levees protect the city from water but those walls are 60 years old unable to handle above a category 2 hurricane. People was experiencing popping in both ears which is a sign from nature that a powerful hurricane is coming toward you. With a high pressure system with a force of nature of surprises.

It's the afternoon before the hurricane, and Katrina was approaching the city of New Orleans on a quiet Sunday afternoon, with huge ominous clouds forming above in the sky every minute, soon to explode into the most dangerous hurricane phenomenon in American history.

At 4:00 pm on August 28, 2005 My neighbor that has a large 3 story tower house that's nearly 50 feet tall came to my house and said the lord sent her with a message, which is for me to leave my house at once because all single dwellings will be destroyed, then she said the lord is watching over you, to protect you, because he love you, so without procrastination I obeyed that message which was delivered by a messenger my neighbor Barbara.

Moments later I'm there at the tower house among several others, Barbara ask me to be in charge of rescue plans, I said yes and notice we did not have an entrance leading to the third floor level which is 35 feet above sea level, which is high enough to be very safe up there.

The local news told New Orleans the water flood level will reach up to 6 feet high, he holy spirit told me Alvin Jacques 12 hours before hurricane Katrina touch down on New Orleans the water flood level will reach up to 18 feet in his neighborhood area and the holy spirit was absolutely correct, Alvin knew ahead of time.

Moments later

I went back home to get a ladder an a spade shovel to make an entrance from the second floor level to the third floor level, hours later I built a hole in the ceiling of second level and we are now inside the third floor level, the storm surge to come may get up to 18 feet above sea level, but we are at 35 feet above sea level out of harms way.

Then moments later I made another hole in the roof top for extra security measures, I was guided by the Lord. To do it several hour before Katrina arrived, to love thy neighbor as thy self, and be prepared hours ahead of time, we were in God's hands mean while on the highways and intersections people are trap, traffic is at a complete stop, vehicles are out of gas blocking traffic in all directions creating explosive chaos, while Katrina get closer to the city and time is running out.

Throughout Louisiana many are experiencing the most dramatic period they have ever seen, the intensity of this hurricane was creating high levels of psychological discomfort. Which put many people into a mental storm of thinking.

The city of New Orleans is left to protect and provide for themselves, it was a quest of the blind leading the blind in fear of a monster category 5 hurricane coming to kill and destroy everything with no limit of high velocity power.

The scope of the storm is making it impossible for anyone to leave without getting trap inside obstacles of dramatic mystery forces. No place is safe to run or hide, this could be the last time for many to be alive, and time is running out as the storm get's closer.

Many people around the world are awaiting the mystery to unfold, New Orleans is inside the big trap of cataclysmic strategy, in a situation as this you can feel the pressures of darkness coming into view, everything was chaotic and the crisis is just beginning, this will be a restless time to be trap beyond your control I'm hoping our steps ahead will be safe for us. With time on our side.

I notice the clouds above is of thunderbolt conditions like a giant firework show in the sky. I know I may not see my house again because nature cannot be controlled which is the biggest nightmare and many people will die, this may be the end of the world for many lives the city is at a crossroad in life

In reality the big wheel in the sky keep on turning and we don't know were we will be tomorrow, life is a mystery that only time will tell the answer the new horizon of a new beginning is on it's way to the point of no return, these compelling ordeals to come may change science fiction into a baby because panic is the worst element a human being can experience, Panic can stop everything from working, and ain't no stopping a supernatural master disaster in action

Katrina is a cataclysmic giant tearing the gulf coast region apart she's closer than we thought 60 percent of the people in New Orleans own there properties, 70 percent are afro Americans and 80 percent do not have insurance to cover there damages, and the big storm will create a metamorphosis throughout the city and surroundings and things will change forever to another dimension

Katrina will show many people throughout the gulf region a new meaning of restlessness for a long time to come, this storm is predicted to bring the ultimate in adversity which is a shocking reality in the night, don't ever under estimate the power of nature in action, Nature has a brain beyond our comprehension of knowledge.

The third floor of the tower house has doors in front of the glass windows, the second and first floors do not have doors in front of the glass windows and the wind surge is now breaking the window glasses on the lower floors

At 1:00 am August 29, 2005 we can feel the winds surging throughout the neighborhood it's breaking roof tops off the other homes, to fly away in the wind, our neighborhoods were beaten hard, but the tower house is passing the test of extreme measure, Katrina was the strongest hurricane in the history of New Orleans and surroundings, Katrina was the most compelling and popular storm of the twenty first century, and Katrina was louder then a freight train driving through thunder, so extreme we could not hear each other talk to one another, the storm's roar was deafening

Monday August 29, 2005 at 2:00 am Katrina starts to hit with energy she is a Catastrophic category 3 at land fall alone the Louisiana and Mississippi coast lines

Her winds roar through dark neighborhoods at lease 1 million residence have move out of these areas but many others are riding out Katrina in there homes, but this is were they will stay and Katrina is there and time has run out for them, they were in a deadly zone.

August 29, 2005 at 4:00 am the nightmare is real the assault of Katrina winds is at 150 miles per hour, that can push a storm surge between 14 to 17 feet high in Louisiana and more is yet to come, she's not finish

At 4:30 am a levee break before the storm fully arrive, at 5:00 am the city looses electrical power and the superdome go's dark the dome has backup generators but they perform reduce lighting and 10 thousand people are inside the dome, and more are arriving. And soon the superdome will have 20 thousand people inside as the storm get's stronger and stronger.

At 6:00 am Katrina was between a Category 3 and 4 Katrina ripe a 15 foot long section of the superdome roof, the eye of the hurricane was south of New Orleans, the ninth ward was flooded from the east and west due to canal walls that collapse.

At 7:30 am intense flooding was pouring in from the east intercostal canals, at 7:30 am Katrina continues to tear away at the roof of the superdome.

At 7:45 am the storm surge alone the industrial canal is pushing pressure against the walls allowing the water to get under the levee foundation to flood the city

Alone the eastern side the industrial canal the ninth ward is flooded rapidly with 18 foot wall of water pouring into those areas destroying houses for blocks which was the most catastrophic rise in the levee breach those people were eye to eye and face to face with the biggest monster flood in modern history.

August 29, 2005 at 7:50 am At the tower house located in the ninth ward one block away from the Mississippi river levees, a giant rushing mountain of water at 18 feet high with the thrust power of the Tsunami is plummeting throughout our community faster then the speed of comprehension destroyed nearly everything in it's path in rapid proportion, this nightmare is real, the ninth ward area experience the most dynamic proportion in the city we were at the mercy of the levee breach inside the epicenter.

The tower house was built to endure severe winds and floods while other homes were being removed from there foundation this area of town was nearly powerless

The magnitude of this flood would have tears to fall from your eyes, your heart is in your throat, and your mind is racing into panic to see a horrific nightmare come to light before your eyes.

This nightmare appeared like something from outer space, but it wasn't a nightmare, we were eye to eye with reality which made it even more dynamic and compelling, the reality was very intense it was a monster of reality

Before the media, news reporters or journalist knew what was happening, my two eyes was able to see and experience the development of that dynamic history making extraordinary havoc.

It started with that monster storm surge of hurricane Katrina that created that monster flood surge from the levee breach that created that super monster havoc that became the biggest super monster natural disaster in the history of America. Which is monster reality

It was the most dynamic sight a human being could witness, which mean it was the highest level of compelling, it was a rare dimension, of dynamics, it was an execution from the next beyond, you had to be there to know, we were eye to eye with the intensity of cataclysmic death, it was far beyond words can express, from start to finish it was like something sent from outer space

Thanks to God we are lucky to be alive and still have a grip on our minds. So that later I could have a story to tell to the world.

God put me in the situation for a reason, it was to help the other people surrounding me, they could not help themselves to survive, God Bless me with the knowledge and experience to be the example that will save their lives from the dynamic circumstances of hurricane Katrina and the enormous sudden impact of the levee breach flood combination, the feeling of those two disasters was miraculous, mesmerizing, extraordinary, compelling and overwhelmingly dynamic it felt like the beginning of the end.

At this location I was bless and able to save 10 lives from death, their names are Iris, Barbara, Donna, Doris, Darlene, Karen, Jesses, Carl, John and myself Alvin. We were the big 10

The hurricane and the flood had everyone shaken, shattered and delusional several of the females were thinking of committing suicide, due to the intensity of the consequences, but Alvin was able to talk them out of thinking suicidal, Alvin was frighten but couldn't show it, because he was the leader of the pack, it was my strength that kept them from doing something foolish or stupid they were loosing their minds, I kept telling them we will get out of this situation soon, keep the faith, I repeated keep the faith nearly a thousand times, they were going crazy and about to give up and time was running out, God gave Alvin Jacques the maturity to exceed the elements surrounding them, and Jacques kept everyone alive as God told him to do. Amen

The water kept rising
When the water finally took a break it was 20 feet high I saw human bodies floating in the water dead it was a diabolical sight to see, many others were trap in attics, with others on roof tops in shock screaming for help it was dynamic to witness because many people were powerless. Hurricane Katrina and the levee breach equal two catastrophic phenomenon disaster in the day of August 29, 2005 which was well beyond the greatest science fiction thriller, which is in my neighborhood area, & it was a mesmerizing situation of bold reality

For many people that live in 2 story houses had to get out quickly because of the 18 foot wall of water. Was filled with deadly elements, the roof top was the safest place to be. As the water continue to rise. At 9:30 am the worst blow of the Katrina was about to hit New Orleans, the eye of the storm is now northeast of the city as her wind swirl counter clock wise, Katrina pushes a storm surge alone the southside of Lake Ponchatrain. To add to the dynamics occurring the city was drowning in overflow.

The waters were racing into New Orleans from both the 17ᵗʰ street and London Avenue canals, the massive pressure from the storm surge destroys a section of the London avenue canal approximately 425 foot long which races the flood water at a more rapid speed which is a flood surge cascade method into the city.

The Jackson barracks military compound which is down river from the French quarters located in the 9ᵗʰ ward, the force of the flood water surrounded 337 National guard troops with 15 feet of high flood water in less then one half hour,

At 9:45 am Massive pressure from the storm surge pushes the walls alone the 17ᵗʰ street canal to the breaking point the wall burst sending the massive flood water from lake Ponchatrain into the city of New Orleans and surroundings, the enormous force acted like a giant bulldozer pushing everything in front of it such as homes, vehicles and small buildings were lifted and destroyed as the mega flood race in those areas, made them at the mercy of high water continual levels

This flood is a deadly mixture of fast running water, broken power lines, gas leaks, floating cars, up rooted trees, destroyed homes, chemicals and oils. And other forms of debris and various elements

Many people don't realize the massive danger there in, they just add to the confusion surrounding them, the levee breach flood pounded the city of New Orleans and surrounding areas with enormous amounts of high toxic water at 18 feet deep and above in other areas.

It's an incredible example how a monster flood could change the face of the city in such a short period of time and killed thousands of people with the damages in the billions of dollars.

The flood was coming into our neighborhood so rapidly it was far beyond our worst nightmare, it was flooding homes and streets with enormous strength it was a man made disaster of a diabolical nature with extraordinary power. The city was told the flood water could reach up to 6 feet high, but suddenly out of the blue many people were face to face and eye to eye with 18 feet at water by surprise.

The flood has turned the city of New Orleans into a river with a surging torrent beyond belief it tears through the landscape with millions of gallons of water per second, a thousand time faster then it's estimate speed, was said to be the surge amount was enough water to fill several Olympic size swimming pool within several seconds, it was the same as a tsunami.

The water crashes into plant, trees and various debris tearing through every thing it meets, clogging up all the drainage outlets in town, no one could stay ahead of the monster flood from hell.

The combination of major flood water and heavy debris is totally lethal. Can you imagine millions and millions of gallons of water racing into your neighborhood within second, the flood water was steaming and rolling the landscape with extraordinary impact pressure by, the element of surprise can be a very shocking thing, to witness or experience. This was a very dynamic situation it was most compelling and unstoppable.

This is what happens to plants and trees inside a major flood, you don't know at what point in time the plant might give up and tear out of the ground, then once the plant let go from the ground it then becomes debris to travel alone with the flood water which adds to the hidden danger of elements inside the flow

Imagine a large tree floating in the water moving at 20 miles per hour it would be able to crash through a one foot thick concrete cement wall, inside the water trees and large debris is on the loose throughout the city an the situation is getting worse by the minute and all defense systems are in trouble.

The combination of hurricane Katrina and the levee breach flood was nothing less than big big trouble, and far beyond anything New Orleans has ever scene display, it was the ultimate of compelling and we were bless to survive and tell the story of what happen on august 29, 2005

The water was forcing itself into every place imaginable, people were lucky to escape the grip of the elements, it was tossing large heavy objects around as if they were little toys, the power of water is powerful, in my neighborhood which is the epicenter, the water was moving more then 50 miles per hour just like a Tsunami force

The water was moving trailer homes as if they were made of paper, some people didn't have time to think, others had to think very fast, they were thinking how much more water is coming.

The trailers were breaking loose trapping people inside, people were screaming from trailer to trailer for help it was sad but people were drowning as the water born trailers continue slamming into each other with broken electrical wires hidden inside the water added to the consequences of rapid death.

Natural gas lines were also broken filling the air with sulfur which will add to the possibilities of heavy explosions and wide spread fires in the city to add to the mess, of circumstances.

A situation like this could happen anywhere, if your city was to be flooded by the extremities of high water by surprise.

The smell of chlorine was in the air this chemical can destroy the respiratory system of it's victims, chlorine is very nasty the scent of it can put a lump inside a human being throat and make them choke with shortness of breathe.

The oils inside the water had surfaces slippery, the harsh toxic chemical inside the water can burn and discolor human skin within minutes,

The natural gas leaks, the toxic chemicals of all types and the various oils was creating extreme chaos which leads to death.

Later explosions and fires was breaking out inside the city of New Orleans and surroundings which made hundreds of people took photographs of the many fires that took place.

The fire department was unable to handle the increasing amounts of fires and chaos

The coast guards with making the most dangerous rescues in the history of the coast guards of America they were saying prayers before rescuing someone because of the danger and risk surrounding them, the consequences was most dynamic and unpredictable.

Then water levels continue to rise as the problems worsened, it was like a Hollywood disaster film featuring the people of New Orleans, the disaster was a giant puzzle, and dead bodies were floating on top the water graveyard style other dead bodies were beneath heavy tons of debris which will take days, weeks and months to find them all. It a monster reality to know thousands and thousands of people were killed by surprise.

The many people of New Orleans and surroundings was experiencing enormous amounts of stress and panic levels at the highest in the history of America

The aftermath of hurricane Katrina and the flood was extremely difficult to believe it was a harsh reality that was unthinkable, surprising and mesmerizing to the natives of New Orleans while people from all around the world witness on global television the intense enigma that trap and killed many people in New Orleans

In Meterie and St. Bernard those two parishes experience water levels between 22 and 27 feet of explosive walls of water, the water surge wasn't stopping it engulf large structures as if they were made of toys, the monster flood was both catastrophic and cataclysmic for those areas, it was an extraordinary phenomenon.

Many people committed suicide by not knowing what to do, bridges and highways were completely wash out, cars and truck were floating with people trap inside, when people are trap inside floating vehicles it is the main cause of deaths in urban floods around the world.

God put me in this situation to help others stay alive, the holy spirit kept me proactive throughout this diabolical crossroad and Gods favor is guiding me forward in various divine ways.

It's difficult to understand what others were feeling the horrific pressures of dark forces is floating in the atmosphere, surrounding us we are inside a once in a life time dimension it's like a horror movie and we are the targets.

My friends and I were praying for salvation to survive and heal in time, throughout the consequences children are without there parents and parents are without there children, the water has taken control by being out of control it's a mystery controlling our thoughts in our minds, it was a mental battle to cope.

Above in the sky various helicopters are circulating the area watching over the city, we are inside the tower house located in the middle of the epicenter and the epicenter is the most deadliest place of devastation in any disasters.

Inside the united states 80 percent of natural and supernatural disasters are flood related, the power of water has extraordinary amounts of momentum.

Fast moving water can sweep a car off the road with surprising ease, at 62 pounds per cubic foot water weighs a lot more then people realize, it moves with a lot of muscle, each foot of rising water brings 500 pounds of pressure to the side of a car, for example a wave at 8 miles per hour has 4 times the pressure as a wave at 4 miles per hour the pressure multiplies every move of speed upward.

Water is mysterious 12 inches of water could make a car float, which means a flood could make a car loose control, the cities turned into a lake it was the power of water in control, which is beyond human control.

The black water is over topping all canals in New Orleans, when the public was told New Orleans was 80 percent under water it means 250 billion gallon of water was in the city

The city was a big fish bowl it was jaw dropping to see, the power of water is like a wet freight train of destructive flow taking control of everything and leaving nothing behind.

The levee breach flood of New Orleans on August 29, 2005 was the biggest flood disaster of the twenty first century. It's hard to explain there was so much devastation of enormous measures it was complete destruction full of consequences, circumstances complication and confusion of chaotic emotions the aftermath of the levee breach was a dynamic man made brutal war between human beings and the water of mother nature. And nature always wins in the end.

When ever a major flood strikes emergency response resources are critical the flood was so intense the emergency resources are over match, telephone calls were pouring into the city by the thousands, while many struggle to survive.

Dump trucks were helping with emergency missions the city emergency supplies completely ran out, then people were stealing supplies to survive the limitations of those compelling disasters, it was a case of do or die.

People were helping people, like the blind was leading the blind others were rescuing the one's that couldn't rescue themselves, unity was in action.

The intensity of those tragedies few tried to forget it happen, to erase the pain in there minds only to cope outside the reality of the truth the city will never forget the behavior of the acts of survival to stay alive. Many people were without a comfort zone in their lives which will take years for them to recover from, it's a cast of being against the odds.

The average home outside the ninth ward area is drowning in 6 to 9 feet of water, the average home inside the ninth ward area is drowning in between 14 to 18 to 20 feet water.

The levees have not just topside, they were breaking the 17th street canal and the London avenue canal broke rapidly only minutes apart from each other

Officials of all levels were unaware the levee in New Orleans have not just topside but are breaking dynamically and time is running out.

The times Picayon new paper photographer Alex Brandon joins the police team the Sherman brothers to document the search and rescue mission, inside the ninth ward entertainer Fat's domino was rescued from his house, among others throughout the city, and gratitude was immediate

Katrina is now moving to a North East direction her brute force eye wall is on the Mississippi gulf coast lines

At 10:00am Katrina delivers a direct hit on the Louisiana Mississippi coast line borders, Katrina also devastates towns including Slidell, Waveling, Bay St. Louis, Gulf port and others with a mega storm surge of massive proportions.

Katrina had a storm surge which was devastating several directions at the same time.

The mayor of Gulf port Mississippi Brent wars was at his mother's house on his two way radio as he monitors police dispatch by voice.

The mayor of Biloxie Mississippi A.J. Halloway was inside city hall with his family to watch Katrina's deadly assaults on his city

Katrina was swallowing Mobile Alabama in 10 feet of water, all power is gone with no communications

Military Russel Oneray was chief in charge of projects he said the storm attack Louisiana and Mississippi with overwhelming forces, Katrina took out all clement of communication and cut out the road network to tray people in which is a classic military attack, who is to take the enemies eyes and ears out so they can't hear or see, to defend themselves, which means their lives were against all odds

In New Orleans a second break of the London avenue canal was in progress it sent more water surging dramatically into the city, governor Blanco was updating officials to the status of the levee breach.

In New Orleans once Katrina passes the damages is shocking and overwhelming for many to witness. This could happen any where to suddenly come in contact with a man made disaster without warning, which is a reality beyond imagination.

In Mississippi Biloxie and Gulfport took a eyewall direct hit and the Grand Casino was moved 450 feet from it original foundation, inside the surge of Katrina in Mississippi the gambling industry is out of luck so are many thousands of homes, many people there lost everything, many people could not believe there eyes everything was gone within minutes.

In New Orleans on Monday August 29, 2005 at 11:15am my prayers of an epiphany were answered the moment I envision several coast guard team looking for survivors were standing on the top of the staint Claude Bridge road, which is directly in front the tower house less then 25 feet away from us.

Then I screamed for help like tarzan, they heard me and rush to the scene, moments later they had a rescue boat park at the front door of the tower house ready to help us from the compelling consequences in the city.

Then the coast guard team came inside the house to give us instructions on what to do, because dangerous elements was inside the water such as poisonous fish, snakes, eels, alligators and others, it was a swamp filled with the most deadliest creatures in the south.

The coast guard team was very professional and well equip to handle this situation, they had automatic rifles with large telescopes able to see 30 feet underwater.

We came down from the third floor to the second floor which only had several feet of water at waist deep, but they protected us as we boarded the rescue boat which was only feet away. We were dancing in the arms of God

Minutes later everyone in safe inside the rescue boat headed for higher ground, to my surprise CNN World news was filming this rescue mission in action it was being televise live around the world, it was a dynamic day of compelling reality to witness.

Moment later on our way to safety I understand we were inside the hands of God, that kept us resilient throughout these adversities, I'm thankful to be alive to tell my story to the world, thanks to god

Within minutes we arrived to higher ground then CNN reporters wanted to interview us to learn how we survive throughout hurricane Katrina and the deep water, surrounding us. We said it was God that kept us alive. Inside the extremities and the enormities of both disasters that killed many other people, which means we were the blessed ones.

Moment later the coast guards came to me and ask if I knew anyone else in need of rescue, I said yes my other neighbors, it's a family of five in that white double house they may still be there, the attic door is in the rear.

Within seconds the coast guards rush to rescue them minutes later all five were brought to safety without injuries. Then I was thankful to be of help to my neighbors lives

As I was standing on higher ground I was able to see my house underwater and realize it was all gone, I loss everything within 20 minutes never under estimate the power of a disaster intensity.

Soon a large coast guard bus will be talking the survivors from here bringing them to the New Orleans superdome to stay, the bus will travel on a road that was design for them to transport the survivors of Katrina,

Inside the bus we have 14 survivors an 6 coast Guardsmen, moments later the coast guardsmen wanted to tell us some of there testimony that happen throughout Louisiana, they said,

Hurricane Katrina and the levee breach flood was the two deadliest catastrophic disasters in the history of the United States coast guard troops

More than 7 thousand coast guard rescue helicopters teams were brought into the New Orleans area at the time of Hurricane Katrina, 33 thousand people were rescued and the coast guard air base in New Orleans is the busiest in America

On our way to the dome we were thankful to the coast guards for saving our lives they were outstanding professionals and did a job well done, we could see throughout the city the aftermath damages was of enormous proportion, the coast guards estimated the damages to be in the multi billions, the city of New Orleans was in big trouble, the city look like a variety of disasters and things such as, a war zone, a nightmare in hell, a nuclear bomb sight, a science fiction project, a havoc into the next beyond, and a song of death from place to place.

New Orleans is not the same anymore, 80 percent of the city is underwater, dead human bodies were floating on top the water, others were dead trap inside attics, homes, building and tons of debris, this tragedy was a state of massive emergency which was far beyond human comprehension scope, which was a new dimension for the world to witness and a new revelation for modern times in America.

Throughout the surrounding communities of New Orleans, Meterie and Staint Bernard the water levels were between 18 to 27 feet high. Many homes are completely destroyed and blown away, large buildings were shattered to pieces, the injured people have nothing to control the pains and sufferings of misery.

Throughout the surrounding states of Louisiana, Mississippi and Alabama many hurricane Katrina victims have die from delusional apocalyptic consequences and the death rate is reaching super astronomical level minute by minute.

Our ride inside the coast guard rescue bus took 40 minutes to reach the superdome area, we notice large hotels, large monumental structures and surroundings were in unrecognizable conditions, the elements of high velocity touch down here to paralyze these areas, most building will take years to repair. But the city will never be the same

Only moments later we arrived at the superdome, now we are among 20 thousand other Katrina survivors in the same place it's a catastrophic brain storm, due to massive thousands injured which was another disaster for our minds to see and witness people of various backgrounds suffering to death in pain, totally unattended without medical supplies for hours and hours.

The people of New Orleans experience hurricane Katrina, the levee breach flood and the superdome entrapment which equals three catastrophic disasters in the same day on august 29, 2005 which became the most dynamic trio in history. Life on earth is the most phenomenal force of nature, it's ahead of the weather catastrophes.

The evening of August 29,2005 Michiel Brown the director of Fema did not admit to CNN officials that the levee breach was happening because he did not want to create massive panic, the media remained uninformed to the levee break for several more hours, which had many journalist and media to think New Orleans escape catastrophic damages, but the results will become clear in the next 24 hours then the true information will be revealed.

Monday August 29, 2005 was the first day inside the New Orleans superdome, the conditions was dramatic and overwhelming it was a catastrophic zone of your mental ability to survive with nothing to control your pains and sufferings as many peoples lives fell apart beyond human comprehension, the dome was another setback to experience.

The clutterness of 20 thousand people all with various problems was an incredible journey to experience, the superdome was the third case of a state of emergency on August 29, 2005, it was a cornerstone of horror.

I will take you on a 5 to 6 day testimonial witness journey and tell you about the determination it took to live and survive in those conditions, we were in a backward situation

Inside the superdome Katrina survivors were introduce to the element of entrapment, they felt like prisoners in a big place beyond there control. I know from experience everything I will tell you is of truth and facts no matter how intense, cruel or extraordinary it may sound it was the true reality of this tragedy, to say that 20 thousand people adventure setbacks and I was one of them.

Moments later all restrooms in the dome are overflowing sewage waste was rising on the floor which created toxic debris to pile up an travel outside the restroom doors into the hallways where everyone could smell the toxic sewage waste throughout the building.

To make matters worsen a women dress as a maintenance worker poured bleach and ammonia mix together is the ingredients to make mustard gas which is very dangerous to inhale. No one was allowed to go outdoor for fresh air all doors were lock tight, it was a trap.

Due to no running water, with very poor ventilation, and a lack of electrical power, created human body odors to increase at the same time the toxic sewage and mustard gas was increasing too. Which it then became a incredible and poisonous scent to inhale which was choking us and burning our eyes.

The restroom are closed and many are hiding somewhere to have a bowel movement or urine as the fumes continue to escape into the air, and get more intense it was endless traps we had to survive.

The 20,000 survivors inside the superdome had various injuries, contagious diseases, psychological disorders and the list go's on and on.

The body odors inside the building was incredible, the people did not have fresh clothing and the running water and toilets was turned off, the only water available was bottle water, the ventilation system was also turned off, the massive degree of filth was enough to kill a human being, it's a miracle I'm still alive and able to tell what happen.

Hurricane Katrina broke large holes in the roof of the superdome, god made the storm do that, so we could have some form of fresh air to breathe, because all windows and doors in the dome was closed and lock, we knew then the odds was against us, so we prayed and prayed and prayed, God in heaven knew mandated evil forces authorized this massive project.

Although we were eye to eye and face to face with a multitude of deadly obstacles surrounding us, but God did not want all of us to die in that building.

Many of the Katrina survivors in the superdome was mesmerized at the evil forces taking place but our faith and prayers kept us alive to the bitter end, the survivors were restless, in a state of confusion and did not sleep for days, they were being drained of what little they had left, some were unable to take the pressure and died and other were to stubborn to die they were the diehards and the unyielding.

Throughout my six day journey inside the superdome I witness strangers helping strangers and enemies helping enemies, I did not witness any form of violence, disturbance or destruction taking place among one another, the people in the superdome had unity with each other.

Within a 6 day period temptation had several women to get rape because most of the women were attractive and irresistible with no place else to go, but the homosexual and the lesbians were happy the were entertaining each other daily, to make the best of this disaster.

With all the devastation and causalities taking place inside the city of New Orleans the New Orleans police force was authorized by female governor Blanco to shoot and kill anyone caught lutering, I know it's wrong to steal, but they are exceptions to the rule, Mayor Ray Nagen said on national television rescue and relief was not coming fast enough, the city of New Orleans was suffering to death for days and days,

Most of the people lutering were good people, but there homes were completely destroyed and they were living in the streets unattended and homeless, they were injured, hungry, dehydrated, exhausted from the disasters and hoping to get rescued and have a shelter to live in, they were trap with the odds against them.

My name is Alvin Jacques I was one of the chosen few by god to hold the title of heroic survivor, god gave me the fortitude, intelligence and determination to help dozens of survivors to stay alive in various ways throughout Katrina, the flood and the superdome, and that was another reason why I wrote this book of catastrophic encounters and called it catastrophic gumbo

The city of New Orleans was in trouble before hurricane Katrina because conservative forces wanted to basically get rid of the poor blacks and the poor whites and other poor minorities so New Orleans could become smaller and richer and this was the purpose and the invention of the flood from the beginning, it's called politics and the conservative forces are the colossal giants.

Regardless of what the media say's nearly 90 percent of the survivors that was lutering were doing that to find food, water, clean clothes and other necessities to live the city was totally devastated, any many of those people lost everything and was struggling to stay alive.

The people inside the superdome and the convention was lock indoors and not permitted to leave the premises regardless of there health or injury condition, they were cage in like animals, I know from experience I was inside the superdome for 6 days and 20,000 people experience a derisive test against humanity at a time when thousands of people needed help in various ways, the things that happen in New Orleans was an experience to never forget, because it's a part of the history of America.

Throughout the superdome and the convention center many Katrina survivors were dying everyday from various injuries and harsh condition throughout those building and throughout the city.

Day by day and minute by minute many survivors in the city and surrounding was suffering to death in attics, on roof tops and in homes hoping to be rescue before the water kill them.

Hurricane Katrina and the man made flood brought monumental neglect to the city of New Orleans, federal court judge Duvall court ruling said by law of the court the Corp of engineers were guilt for creating that man made flood disasters by failing to maintain the levee, Judge Duvall verdict said not only did the government forsake the people of New Orleans but the government created the disaster in the first place and knew New Orleans and surrounding was headed for a dead end.

The flood of New Orleans was intended to be 3 times bigger than estimated so the conditions would become horrifying and paralyzing the neglectment of the levee was not an act of god it was done on purpose by the army corp of engineers over a period of years.

Katrina was known to change the mind set of human nature, Katrina transformed a rich mentality into a poor mentality for a uncertain period of time, the aftermath of the devastation taught the rich mentality to cope with vision and the circumstances of a poor mentality to survive, until they were able to get back on there feet again.

Here's another way of saying it, Katrina stripe everyone of there superiority, and the enormity of the devastation taught everyone the meaning of humbleness.

The people in the states of Louisiana, Mississippi, Alabama and Florida were face to face with multiple fatalities, and eye to eye with a gumbo mixture of bulleye catastrophics. Katrina killed thousands and thousands of people throughout the gulf coast region.

On Tuesday August 30, 2005 the flood water in New Orleans official covered 80 percent of New Orleans and Katrina has destroyed more then 200 thousand homes as the survivors struggle throughout the city limits

Thousands of desperate residence are trap in there homes face by the rising water in there attics, which then had them to break through roof tops to live as they wait and prayed for help to come.

A depleted New Orleans police force struggle to come to the aid and police will report that 249 policemen deserted there post during the hurricane and yet rescue missions are still in full swing by United States coast guardsmen and the flood water were continually coming into the city of New Orleans and surrounding areas. As chaoticness increase and got worse.

Tuesday August 30, 2005 Michiel Brown the director of Fema told the mayor Ray Nagen of New Orleans he will send 350 to 500 buses there in New Orleans by tomorrow August 31, 2005, but the buses took nearly 3 days to arrive due to high flood water surrounding the superdome

On August 30, 2005 the governor Blanco of New Orleans wanted the 20 thousand evacuees which was in the superdome to be moved to the Houston Astro dome, but the flood water was to high to move them, they were trap in misery and fear

Throughout New Orleans and the nation, people are beginning to wonder what's going on at the dome 20 thousand survivors are awaiting to be rescued and Fema said it will take nearly 455 busses to evacuate the superdome completely. Which means time was running out at the superdome people were going crazy about to loose their minds, and many were very injured, and I was one of them.

Throughout New Orleans, Meterie, Staint Bernard and other surrounding cities look like the middle of the river, & many lost everything

Tuesday August 30, 2005 is the second day for the evacuees in the dome, but many of them have the faith and the determination to get through this nightmare entrapment some way or some how.

Throughout New Orleans vandalism is completely out of control, the governor enforce a rule for police to shoot and stop anyone in the present act of vandalism.

Throughout the city crime is out of control the people are killing one another, other were loosing there minds by shooting at military helicopters in action of rescuing others, the city of New Orleans was totally chaotic, people were going crazy and the consequences didn't stop

Wednesday August 31, 2005 the third day in the superdome, my name is Alvin, several days ago inside Katrina I hit my leg while being rescued, Now I find I'm in need of a medical doctor as soon as possible, my right leg is very infected it has swollen to be twice as big as my left leg, the infection can lead to severe blood poison, which could kill me in time, the pain in my right leg is enormous I need help, now.

Suddenly out of the blue a strange women came to me and said God sent me to you, my name is Joana, I have cancer and the pain is killing me, I don't have my cancer medicine with me to stop the pain, then Joana said God told me if you would only pray with me my cancer pains would stop, then I Alvin said yes Joana I will pray with you to help you.

Then Joana and I put our hands together and bow our head and started to pray in the name of God

Moments later the two of us Joana and I can feel a change coming over our bodies and minds it had to be God, Joana was healing Alvin of the pains in his right leg while at the same time Alvin was healing Joana of her pains of cancer, the unity of praying together with open hearts and sincerity was healing both of us in the name of God.

Joana and I Alvin just experience a unique revelation sent by God from heaven which will help and secure us to endure and enforce us to handle, the big journey ahead of us. Two hours ago Joana and Alvin were complete strangers to each other, and now we have a miraculous testimony to take with us throughout life until the end of time, and with the favor of god in your life the impossible is possible. God can do anything and everything, Amen

August 31, 2005 in Mississippi 12 Casinos were destroyed by hurricane Katrina's storm surge.

August 31, 2005 New Orleans will bring full force chaos of gang rapes and murders throughout the city.

August 31, 2005 the water in Mississippi and Alabama went back to sea but the water in New Orleans created a big bowl of water and the pumping station are out of order, which mean the city will be flooded for a week

The evacuee survivors in New Orleans Know the people in Mississippi and Alabama got help quickly, but the people in New Orleans have to wait a longer time to get help, they were against the odds

Over the next few days Louisiana officials are predicting as much as 10 thousand may be dead throughout the city and surroundings , they were trapped

New Orleans is being disregarded and ignored like this massive disaster is not happening, in other parts of the city of New Orleans heroic survivors were hijacking public buses to rescue other survivor that are trap in need of rescue and bringing them to safety they took a stand to help others

Thursday September 1, 2005 the fourth day in the superdome 20 thousand people were experiencing a diabolical psychological punishment, the survivors are struggling to hold on, many are hurt, weak and still in panic which is killing them, four day of entrapment is enough to make anyone delusional and many were physically injured in need of immediate attention, we need a miracle to stop the misery and pain, that was cast upon us. By this man made element.

This late past due rescue has created an enormity of consequences it was like being inside a big science fiction tank with no way out.

For four day and four nights the army military soldiers kept there fingers on the triggers of there M16 Combat Rifle all day everyday from start to finish, which was a psychological message that told everyone of us to watch your step, the military was ready for action and we the survivors were the targets with no place to run or hide. We were face to face with an enigma between life and death.

Hours later on September 1, 2005 a man step out the crowd and said to me, Hay, Big brother my name is Sam can I talk to you for a moment, I said OK

He said Big Brother I've got a problem, Katrina took my house, my wife and my family, I don't know what to do, I have gun, I feel like killing someone because I'm in pain, Big Brother what should I do.

I said everyone in here got a problem look around you everybody's in pain your not alone.

I said that man on the floor is having a heart attack, he loss 2 houses and his family is dead, his name is Sam with a problem.

I said that women is having a stoke, she loss 3 houses and her 6 children are dead, her name is Sam with a problem

I said look at me, I lost my house, my family, my mother, I'm about to loose my leg it's infected, and my name is Sam with a problem.

I said all of us have the same thing in common, everyone is Sam and our pains and sufferings, is the same inside the superdome

Then the real Sam said, Big Brother thank you for the coffee I understand everybody is in trouble in here with the same needs.

I said to Sam be cool man, make the best of your day

Some times a person with a problem can feel better when they know others have problems too. The world is filled with many problems, no one is alone that have a problem.

It's not what happen to you is the problem it's how you feel about what happen to you can eliminate the problem can become negative or positive the decision is yours but if you think differently you can live differently, you will never loose every think if you keep your mind together, it's called the power of reasoning

The New Orleans French quarters have been spared by flood water which means most of the French quarters remains dry, here's the reason it's a combination of higher ground earth and effective levee board alone the Mississippi river kept the water out of the French quarters.

While most of the city of New Orleans faces two major crisis which is how do they stop the water from pouring in, and how do they get the water out. The neighborhoods many people were spellbound.

In Mississippi and Alabama and other cities water drains naturally even in low line area, but not in New Orleans, most of New Orleans is 6 feet below sea level which is like a bowl, the New Orleans bowl traps water so every drop has to be pump out of the city, the city solved that problem years ago with massive series of 22 pumping station throughout the city area.

The pumping stations are located at drainage canals that empty into Lake Ponchatrain, the 22 city pumps operate the same as a home version pump operates, these pumps trigger automatically by rising water which is more advance then the pumps in our basements at home.

The larger version pumps are called drainage pumps, the 148 drainage pumps are capable of pumping extreme amounts of water, they can drain a Olympic size swimming pool in just seconds.

Drainage pumps can pump out 30 billion gallons of water a day which is more then one million liters per second which is enough to fill up the superdome building within 35 minutes, or less.

But the 22 pumping stations and the148 drainage pumps are useless until the big holes in the levees are fix, nothing will get done.

Which means all the water pump out the canals would leak back into the city due to the levee breaches, massive slabs of solid concrete and three thousand pounds of large sand bags was being used to block the pouring water of the levee breach, this was the first desperate attempt to plug the holes

Those holes are big holes to fill in 3 locations, the 17th street canal, the London avenue canal and the industrial canal.

But why did the levees breach and could there failure hold the secret to saving New Orleans from future calamities.

August 31 and September 2, 2005 flood risings was at a slower pace when the level of water in the city match up with the level of Lake Ponchatrain, 80 percent of New Orleans is now a toxic Lake of 250 billion gallons of water, which will take several weeks to pump it out of the city, the drowning of New Orleans was a man made disaster.

Friday September 2, 2005 is the fifth day for the survivors inside the superdome, they are still waiting for Fema buses to rescue them from the nightmare of this great calamity in the United States of American history.

As of September 2, 2005 10 females of women and young girls were rape by gangs throughout the superdome within a five day period.

Then at 10:00 pm in the superdome three women stood up and made an announcement to the crowd around them, they wanted to have an orgy with any man available, within minutes men are standing in line with there penis erected, they were looking forward to this orgy, within several hours the orgy increase to more than one hundred people actively involved in pleasure, the orgy lasted from 10:00 pm September 2 until 3:00 am the next morning, many people at the superdome were completely surprise an orgy was taking place at a time like this.

Then someone found alcohol in one of the storages of the dome, then everyone begin to get drunk it was a party of sex and alcohol, that last until 5:00 am then everyone got tired and weak and returned to there seats to sleep, the fun for them was done, the party was over.
3 hours later
At 8:00 am something burst open in the building which was sending heavy toxic gases into the air it was difficult to breath the oxygen was depleted, people were chocking and gasping for breathe as they stampeded out the building like cattle, the military wanted us out of the building immediately, they the departure buses will be coming soon, which took more then seven hours later. To show up.

Within the 20 thousand survivors in the superdome only about two hundred were actively involved with that orgy, and now everyone is having to pay the price for those who were part of the orgy, our lives will be in jeopardy because the military is piss off.

As we the survivors waited for rescue buses, many survivors were put to strenuous work by military request, as they struggle to survive in misery.

The army military wanted 40 survivors to design six separate different departure lines put in single file formations by using one hundred 6 foot long steal barricade barriers to do it

These six departure lines will disburse the Katrina survivors into 44 various states nation wide throughout America, which will create thousand of families to be separated from one another with no means of communication, which is the worst that could happen at a time like this

The military then said to the survivors of the work is not done on time, it will delay your departures to leave town so get the work done immediately, because hurricane Rita is coming to New Orleans at a catastrophic proportion and we will leave all of you here to drown, so get to work now, and don't get stupid.

We the survivors were already at attention to obey the army military, because the army solider kept there fingers on the triggers of there M16 Combat rifles throughout the entire stay at the superdome, to keep us on our toe's, which made us feel like we were living on the edge of time, and time was running out, while the military played with our minds and kept us in psychological discomfort the Katrina survivors were in great fear of there lives, so they did as they were told. With the odds against them day by day for five days continuously. They were sent to wipe us out. This was a horrifying journey for everyone to witness and experience, our army troops kept us in fear of being killed, we knew our lives was in severe jeopardy of great consequences and several hours later the work is done and finish, now it's time to disburse 20 thousand Katrina survivors into 44 various states throughout America.

One hour later on September 2, 2005 the first set of buses arrived at 3:00 pm, only women and children were allowed to board the buses, my lady friend Iris boarded that bus to Houston texas, the others were left behind, as families were being sepearated.

The second set of buses arrived at 6:00 pm, more women, children and elderly boarded the buses, the man were left behind to wait, as more families and couples were separated in this calamity.

The third set of buses arrived at 10:00pm, the last of women, children and elderly, as the men still wait in pain and sorrow.

The fourth set of buses arrived at 1:30am the next day September 3, 2005 which was my bus, this bus was headed to Dallas Texas as others waited behind, for the next set of buses so they could board.

It was a 10 hour ride from New Orleans to Dallas and all means of communication was out of order for months, due to the cell phone master towers were destroyed.

Many children are separated from there families and many families are separated from there children, it was chaotic without communication from your love one's.

Days later
After departures for days, weeks and months many New Orleans families are separated from each other with no means of communication of transportation many cell phone tower were destroyed and broken throughout the southern region in wait of repair

In late September 2005 the citizens of Katrina went into the four corners of the globe misidentified on national television as foreign refugees, with no relationship or family, they were disburse throughout 44 various states inside America to provide and flourish for themselves after a massive series of crisis in New Orleans.

This situation was a morality play witness by people all around the world as they watch what Katrina, and the levee breach and the superdome did the native New Orleanians, on August 29, through Sept. 2, 2005

This series of calamities which occurred is a wake up call for America to do a better job of unity on earth for God, and stop the hate for one another.

It's 10:00am September 3, 2005 I've been riding this bus for about 8 hours, alone the way the bus made a stop at a rest park, where emergency medical crew came into the bus and said, is anyone injured, I raised my hand and said, I need help to walk I can't walk anymore, in a flash 5 medical members were carrying me off the bus and put me into an ambulance, where I was examine, then rush immediately to Marshall regional hospital which is a hospital for the rich and famous, located in Marshall Texas it's a hospital with exceptional gifted doctors on staff, which is also one of the best hospitals in America.

I'm very bless to be in the right place at the right time to get the right treatment and attention, thanks to God, Amen.

It's been 7 days since I had a good sleep, I looking forward to rest time, being at this hospital today is grace sent to me from above that shines upon me, the heavens above gave me the strength and a good mind to endure those incredible ordeals of extraordinary forces and miraculous impacts that had New Orleans in mesmerizing consequences.

This is my very first time being a passenger patient inside an ambulance, within moment we have arrived at Marshall regional hospital, a team of doctors are awaiting me at the doors of the emergency room, soon as I was taken from the ambulance, they immediately started cutting all my clothes off my body, to prepare me for emergency service, thanks to God. I'm a blessed man, Amen.

Later that evening the staff ask me would I please tell them some stories of what happen, the story I told them, made tears fall from there eyes, my hospital room was filled with hospital staff, they comfort me 24 hours a day and was very professional all the way.

September 4, 2005 the second day in the hospital, my doctors think it's a miracle, I'm still alive able to function with all the toxic poisons inside my body, I have not made a bowel movement in 7 days, I'm full of back up poisons, due to the stress of a series of calamities which was getting the best of me psychologically, internally and physically.

September 5, 2005 the third day in the hospital, I awaken that morning with six separate IV needles attach to my body, which were two pain killers, two blood thinners, and two antibiotics to keep my right leg from being amputated, for a moment, I thought I was dreaming with six IV in me, but I've been living on the edge for 8 days without medical attention, I was bless to be alive, I was in severe pain days ago, but I had to cope and strive with faith in my heart believing brighter days were ahead of me, and to deal with those ordeals took, extraordinary strength, Amen

September 6, 2005 the Fourth day in the hospital the poisons inside of me took control over the medicines, the doctor increase my dosage 4 times for the medicines to take a grip, the poisons increase my waist line by 10 inches in 9 days I went from a size 42 waist to a size 52 waist line I had massive bloat blowing me up big time and extremely fast.

Today I'm having my first bowel moment in 9 days and what a relief it is, the poison is coming out, and tomorrow will bring better results.

September 7, 2005 the fifth day in the hospital, I am caught off guard a priests by the name of Father Denzell came into my hospital room to give me holy communion and the last rights, he said I may die in 4 hours, I said that's incredible I don't fell bad enough to die, it's not time for me to die, I can feel it in my heart I will stay alive.

The priest said faith is to be certain of the uncertainties in life, I said I certain I'm not ready to die, the priest said mister Jacques I see you're a very determine man, I said yes I determine to live.

The priest said 10 years ago I almost die but my faith kept me alive to tell my story to others, there's no limit to the power of God, he said mister Jacques I can see god in your eyes, God is in the center of your life at this time, I said yes I agree
Then the priest said mister Jacques I think you will be ok, I said thank you father Denzel, the priest said make the best of your day mister Jacques, I said thank you father Denzel, then I fold my arms and prayed myself to sleep; several hours later my doctor walk in and said my health is out of the danger zone, I said thank you God, and thank you Doctor for that report. My health was improving at last.

Then my doctor James C. Logan said it's getting later mister Jacques, I'll see you tomorrow, I said good night doctor, I'll see you tomorrow as well

September 8, 2005 I'm feeling much better today, the staff here at the hospital would like to give me a recovery party, they were very kind to me.

One hour later we are having a party in my hospital room, staff an visitors was attending, they wanted my autograph for being a Katrina survivor and a hero that saved many others lives

Later at the end of the party, I thank everyone there for being good humanitarians and professionals, they told me thank you mister Jacques, I said your welcome it's a pleasure being here at Marshall regional hospital

Several hours later my doctor and nurses were in my room telling me of my update health report, they said I was doing excellent but very bless to be alive after what I've been through, I said thank you very much for the encouragement, then we said good night to each other, then I fell asleep.

One hour later at 11:00 pm the telephone rings, it's two family members my sister and brother calling on a three way connection, she lives in Washington, he lives in Atlanta, they called to tell with sorrow in there hearts, Our mother Mrs Dorothy Angelety Jacques drowned to death in the flood of New Orleans,

I said to them be strong and gave them encouragement, maturity and support, then I prayed with them, they were looking up to me to give them strength because I'm Big Brother, so I surrendered and lovingly gave them all I had, to make them feel better, with comfort they needed support from me, which made me feel like superman because I'm in the hospital.

I felt honored to help my sister and brother in a time of need, Katrina shook everyone in one way or another, I have eight sisters and one brother, I hope the others are able to cope, then I prayed in my mother's behalf, then meditated until I fell to sleep. Because God have my mother Mrs. Dorothy Jacques in a better place in time

Friday September 9, 2005 today is my last and final day in the hospital, I'll be checking out at 4:00pm which is several hours away, I have family members that live in the Marshall Texas area, they will be picking me up at 4:00pm, and I'll be staying with them for a few days to visit and take it easy.

At 4:00pm my relative are at the hospital it's good seeing them, we have a lot to talk about, moments later we arrived at there home, they have a lovely home in Texas, with a huge back yard, with lot's of trees and plants, with lot's of outdoor furniture, and the house is made of Brick, with 10 large rooms, it a beautiful place to live.
Later we had dinner and talk about many things for hours, then other relatives came over to share sometime with us, we were growing together as the time slip away.

It's 2:00am in the morning of the next day, which is time for us to get some sleep, we said good night to each other and drift off to sleep.

September 10, 2005 everybody had a good nights rest, our names are, Isadore, Grace, Meme, GeGe, David, Peter, and Alvin, I'm thankful I had good relatives in Marshall Texas to help me moments me.
Moments later
We had a good lunch to eat, then we drove around the city to sight see for several hours then we returned home to watch some movies to have a good time with each other all night long, it been years since we have been together.
The next day Saturday September 11, 2005 we had a picnic all day outdoors in there huge back yard with lot's of nature trees surrounding us and the weather was beautiful from morning to night, the food is good and the company is great, we are family.

Then I had a chance to contact my lady friend Iris she was staying in Houston Texas with her relatives, we were separate inside the departures, we made plans to see each other very soon some time tomorrow, we have a lot to talk about, we were together throughout Katrina, the flood and the superdome, both of us are very lucky to be alive, she did not get physically injured, but both of us were mentally shaken by those ordeals, of miraculous proportions

Sunday September 12, 2005 my relatives and I went to church then we had a buffet dinner at a local restaurant, the food was good, then we returned home, soon I'll be catching a Greyhound bus for Houston Texas, David will be bringing me to the bus station, it time to say goodbye to everyone, it's time to go and I'll see them again soon.

The ride from Marshall Texas to Houston Texas is five hours long, while in transit to Houston, I had time to think about my journey ahead of me, life is full of mysteries, I'm thankful I've been able to cope with adversity and have a testimony to tell the world how I endured the unbelievable.

In a few minutes my bus will be arriving inside Greyhound bus station of Houston Texas, the bus ride is coming to a end

Now the bus is park inside the station, I'm getting my luggage together to meet Iris, in the seating area, meanwhile Iris is there waiting on me with open arms, we have not seen each other in ten days, we have some catching up to do.

Iris brought two cousins with her, named Nat and Lynn, we will be staying with them for several days, her cousins think I'm a nice guy because I was able to save Iris life inside those ordeals in New Orleans.

Iris and I feel good to be together again, now we can make plans for the future as time go's on, Iris said to me it's a big relief seeing me, I said I feel that same way about you too.

Then I said now it's time the think beyond yesterday, so we can prepare for tomorrow with clarity.

Moments later we have arrived at Nat and Lynn home, they have a beautiful place here in Houston, with a big front yard filled with all types of plants, the house is made of brick with 8 large rooms of various color with all the comfort of home.

Nat and Lynn have three vehicle, a truck and two cars, they let Iris use one of the cars, I had the truck and Nat and Lynn used the other car, all of us had transportation to get around the Houston area and shop for necessities. And that made us feel very welcome to be with them.

The next day
Monday September 13, 2005 most of the day Iris and I stood home to plan where will we go from here, most of the people we know in New Orleans are gone, they evacuated to who knows where, Iris have a daughter that lives in Philadelphia and she would like us to come there, we know Philadelphia is far away from Houston or New Orleans, but sooner or later we must find a place for us to be comfortable, far away from hurricanes and floods and tornados,

New Orleans is the hurricane and flood city, and Texas is the tornado and flood city which means the further away, the better, only time will give us the answer, we need time to heal from catastrophic ordeals, the aftermaths of Katrina was enough for a lifetime, and Texas, Oklahoma and Arkansas is inside of Tornado Alley, and Tornado Alley harbors more than 400 twisters yearly. Which is a bit much for us at this time, we need less excitement in our lives.

No one had a clue the aftermath of Katrina would put the city of New Orleans under 80 percent of toxic water filled with hundreds of poisonous chemical of all types, also filled with other types of poisonous fish, eels, snakes, alligators it was truly a serious death trap.

The problems and chaos throughout the city was unthinkable, it was far beyond anything over seen in the country of America, it was under a foreign demon force, which was beyond the worst nightmare to survive.

In mid September of 2005 Iris and Alvin were still in Houston Texas having a good time at Nat and Lynn's house, but in New Orleans hurricane Rita came to town and reflooded and redamage the city for a second time, the flood water is several feet higher and more properties are damage and the city is in deeper chaos.

The city of New Orleans is now between 80 to 90 percent under water, as the death rates increase in delusion of a second storm havoc in the same location, which was the worst set a hurricane natural disasters in American history.

September 23, 2005 tonight is our last night in Houston Texas, Iris and I have had a very good time here and may come back some day to visit, but tomorrow morning at 6:00am Iris and I will be headed for Philadelphia PA. the city of Brotherly Love.

It's 3:00 am we are getting ready to leave, one hour later, we arrived at the airport, then we were transported around the airport in special small car design to travel throughout the Houston airport.

Now it's 6:00 am time to board the plane our flight will be arriving in Philadelphia at 10:00 am within 4 hours.

In the pass I've had opportunity to travel around the world with various musical groups as a drummer entertainer, but I've never been to Philadelphia Pennsylvania. Which was the former capital of the United States of America, before Washington D.C. became the capital headquarters.

4 hours later we are landing in Philadelphia on schedule the city of brotherly love, the airport is one of the largest in the country of America

Moment later the two of us are inside the airport looking for a philly cheese steak, which should be easy to find in Philadelphia.

My friend Iris thought it would be a good idea for me to stay with her at her daughters house for a while until I got my own place organize

Her daughter will be picking us up in 30 minutes, then after leaving the airport we stop to eat at old country buffet, then we went to her daughter house to relax and settle down for the night.

The weather in Philadelphia is nice and cool in September which is good for us, Philadelphia is my new home to discover and explore in new development of peace and love, with a feeling of autumn in the air, I know winter is coming soon, which is my favorite time of the year, and I hope Philadelphia make us happy hear, because this is our new home.

The next day while taking a walk around the neighborhood, I found a car just right for me, a Taurus GL wagon now I have a car to find an apartment and get around the city, I think time is on my side.

Days later I found the right apartment at Lynnewood garden's in Elkins park PA., soon I'll be moving into the place, so I can focus clearly on my new life in a new city, which is away from the psychological discomforts of the pass.

I know I must start my life all over again, somehow it may do me good, because in New Orleans, within 20 minutes I loss everything I owned in the levee breach flood due to hurricane Katrina. Now it's time to start a new life and a new attitude to become better then before with the help of God. I can do all things through god who strengthens me.

Two days later I'm inside the apartment, it feels good, finally I have private time to myself with privacy to heal and think about the future.

The city of brotherly love was an asset to the Katrina survivors, between 5 and 10 thousand survivors came to Pennsylvania to escape the consequences in New Orleans.

Special thanks to Gene Schmolze, Clair Dale, Susy Sourwall, Katrina Pratt, George Romero, and others for a job well done of helping the Katrina survivors to reestablishing themselves in Pennsylvania

I moved into this apartment on Halloween night of 2005, the apartment sits on the corner first in line, my car is park only feet away, I have a view of the Cheltenham shopping mall which is directly across the street. I also have a view of the traffic intersection from the apartment.

Elkins Park is a safe community it sits side by side to Philadelphia, the neighbors are friendly and I like location and surroundings

Several months ago I came to Philadelphia from Texas with only the clothes on my back, to get away from New Orleans because everything I owned was gone, I was hoping and looking toward to regain my independence and clarity in a better way, because I have good momentum and want to be stronger then before, and better then ever I've been blessed, I have a place to stay, transportation, furniture, my health is doing much better and things are looking better for me, this is my first time in Pennsylvania and I was told it gets very cold here in the winter time, it one of the coldest states in America.

It's 3 months after Katrina, I'm in my apartment all alone by myself, in my mind sometimes I think about the transformation I made from New Orleans to Philadelphia it happened from out of the blue without preparance or preparation, I made a lucky wise decision and landed in Philadelphia Pennsylvania to reset myself.

Suddenly I was given a new life, in a new city with new surroundings among new people, I was transpose by god to discover and develop the other side of me to become a brand new butterfly in Philadelphia

Being alone in a new place sometimes I administer to myself, sometimes I advocate to myself and sometimes I just think about my life to myself to keep my faith in action, faith is the opposite of evil, I love myself so I don't give up on my dreams of tomorrow, faith can make the impossible become possible, my faith can make the impossible become possible, my faith in god is my secret weapon when all odds are against me.

I think God put me in Philadelphia Pennsylvania to pull my life together and write a series of books about the extraordinary dynamic catastrophic consequences from America to around the world and have it to be one of the best series books ever written.

Taking time to research my new surrounding I discover Pennsylvania have a population of 12.5 million people

1. While being here several months I learned 70 percent of the pharmaceuticals in America are made in Pennsylvania

2. The largest shell oil refinery of the north east is in Pennsylvania

3. Fairmount Park in Pennsylvania is the largest park in the world it has a city built inside the park as an added feature.

4. The Betsy Ross bridge in Philadelphia has dedicated to her for her outstanding creation of the American flag and Betsy Ross was also the first inventor of ice cream.

5. Pennsylvania was the first state capital of America, then came Washington D.C. the declaration of independence and the Liberty Bell is located in mid town Philadelphia

6. Germantown Pennsylvania was built by the Germans of Germany years ago. It's a historic place to see. That's relative to Europe.

Here's six examples of trust of faith I accomplish while being in Elkin's Park PA. the summit of development

1. No matter how bad your life could get just don't give up on your tomorrow trust in gods new ideas.

2. God has taken me out of wicked deadly disaster of the dark and gave me hope in Elkins Park to develop.

3. God repaired my right leg by putting life and action back into the cells that was once dead for a better life

4. the aftermath of Katrina took it all, God taught me to stand firm and tall and except I once lost it all, and once I was blind but now I can see, that god is the only one protecting me.

5. I learned the power of answers is in gods hands god can see before you to guide and watch your steps ahead, the impossible is possible be an artist of maturity, attitude and momentum.

6. God made us to love him and love one another in unity of opposites, it will be as full of light as when a lamp gives you light with it's rays - luck 11:36 Get to know your heart and stay open to prospective of creativeness

In my Journey of being in Elkin's park PA. I had the opportunity to go to a good hospital to get a complete check up.

The doctor at this hospital wanted me to loose weight, so he used psychology on me to make a long story short his psychology work, I lost 80 pounds, after all was said and done I thank the doctor for the push forward.

Then I was able to do things like I was much younger to be at my best

Special thanks to Dortor Mortomer Stronge at Albert Einstein of Elkins Park PA.

Now I am presently at St. Catherine Medical clinic my health is in top shape the staff is very professional

Special thanks to Dr. Davies, Dr. Katherine, Nurse Gene and Nurse Rosemary for keeping me in check at St. Catherine medical clinic in German town PA.

By being an entertainer I knew Philadelphia has musical celebrities like Grover Washington, the O Jays, Pattie Labell, Boney James and many others, that live and perform here.

Inside center city I was able to hear other musical groups playing Jazz, Blues, Latin and other types of music, I was well entertained, and will return to hear more music again

Moving to Philadelphia from New Orleans I learned both places have tourism in common people visits various parts of the city because of it's uniqueness

I have been a drummer for 40 years and a lead vocalist for 30 years, I've travel and recorded with various entertainers from around the world throughout the years of my performances.

I've had a very popular band in New Orleans by the name of the Alvin Jacques international trio plus the group is no longer together because of Katrina everyone lives in a different city and states at this time maybe some day we will be together again, Katrina give many people a New life to live in a different place and location.

Mr. Alvin Jacques is the author of this book entitle Catastrophic Gumbo he is 56 years develop and matured to express himself, God has given him the opportunity to be a business man, professional drummer, percussionist and lead vocalist among other gifts & talents for over 40 years.

Mr. Jacques has traveled and recorded around the world to over 100 countries internationally in which he has performed with various legendary entertainers throughout Europe, Asia, the Caribbean, South America and the United States

Mr Jacques has also had the opportunity to have received endorsements by various drum and drum stick companies, he has performed in over 15 major hotels in the New Orleans area with his band the Alvin Jacques international trio plus for many years, New Orleans have been good to him, from Jacques with love to New Orleans.

But hurricane Katrina change the city of New Orleans to another place for a while, Jacques had a lot of good memories of New Orleans, it's his original home town, Jacques is presently developing new creations for a new come back. To be more dynamic then ever, his maturity level is much greater.

Some of the best entertainers in the world are from New Orleans, these groups include Fat's Domino, Harry Connick Jr, the Neville Brother, the Marcellus Family, Professor longhair, Jean Knight King Floyd, Tommy Ridgley, Jonny Adams and many many others which includes Actors, Daneers, Writers and business people of the musical world.

Mr. Alvin Jacques professional career started at age of sixteen in 1970

The original city of New Orleans was filled with Jazz, Afro Cuba, Blues, Caribbean Latin and other exotic sounds from around the world, the musicians of New Orleans played in various unique forms.

New Orleans will continue to have a Mardi Gras, New Orleans was founded in 1718, the first cemetery was built in 1789, and the first Voodoo Queen of New Orleans was Marie Labo, and throughout America 150 million people believe in ghost and Voodoo.

Today my youngest sister Darlene Jacques Hutchson called to say, New Orleans is sending me two brand new sets of drums as a gift of appreciation for being a Entertainer Musical roll model in New Orleans, I said that's a wonderful gift tell them thank you very much indeed.

Darlene called back the next day and said the manager of the project Juan Labostra want to know your favorite color, I said emerald green. Darlene said the manager going to send you the drums, cymbals, hardware and the Luggage cases. I said that's as good as it gets, it's a total package. Thanks again

Several weeks later everything arrived at my apartment, in Pennsylvania the drums are miraculously beautiful everything was top flight material equipment. I'm a blessed man for knowing good people throughout New Orleans.

Special thank you to my lovely sister and her daughter Darlene and Christeen Hutchison and the hi tech drum company for the lovely drums.

Special thank you also to Juan Labostra, New Orleans and the taye drum Company for the lovely drums.

I'm thinking everyone for there consideration and generosity, from Jacques with love to New Orleans and friends and all the beautiful times I've had there, it's a city I'll never forget it's the birth place of Jazz, with various types of music from around the world.

Today my youngest brother Anthony Jacques is coming to visit me in Pennsylvania from Atlanta

He will be arriving a 4:00 PM when he get here I'll take him out to eat at old country buffet in Elkins park which is only a few blocks away

Anthony like the Elkins park area of Pennsylvania, I'm sure we will have a good time, he and I love to eat good and both of us like fish, smash potatoes and salad, with cheese cake and ice yoga for desert, the food at the buffet is pretty good

After we get sometime to eat, he and I will take a ride around the city then he and I will come back to the apartment to listen to some good music and watch television for the night.

The next morning we had a good breakfast before he left for Atlanta then 6 hours later Anthony called me to say he arrived in Atlanta safely, Anthony and I will hook up again in a few week until next time, see ya

My faith before hurricane Katrina was strong which is the reason how I am still alive today with a miraculous testimony of survival in major adversity to share with the world, which is never under estimate the power of a natural and supernatural disaster.

December 2005 is 3 months after Hurricane Katrina and hurricane Rita, the true reality in New Orleans is many people do not know where there families, friends, neighbors or love ones are anymore since Katrina, many people were separated from one another, many wish there nightmares would just go away and never come back, easy said then done.

But a harsh reality is stronger than a human mentality regardless of the self control of a person mind, it's a psychological discomfort to have no control over the mysteries of consequences, our lives could change in a flash, due to unforeseen circumstances beyond our control.

Life is the strongest entity of the forces of nature on earth. Life is the supernatural ultimate of survival and the most colorful source of energy on earth

Life is a mystery beyond the theory of history, man is still searching for answers for things that happen yesterday.

My faith in god was my secret weapon when all odds was against me, I let go and let god do it all and my life becomes better in many ways.

In December of 2005 the condition in New Orleans has worsen as time go's on, many survivor are homeless, living and suffering in the street without shelter, others are in tents outside the doors of city hall trying to seek assistance to stay alive.

Throughout the city homeowners and residences are still without running water, electrical power, phone service, internet service, gas in homes, plus no hospital are open, no medical aid available, no transportation is in service which means the city is suffering in setbacks

Taboo Aftermath

At the peak of destruction in December no green leafs are on the trees, and the poison water left an odor that wouldn't leave the city of New Orleans and surroundings.

In New Orleans and surrounding Katrina's storm surge was phenomenal, but the levee breach flood surge was astronomical within 20 minutes the harm was done. Nearly 80 percent of natural disasters worldwide are flood and tsunami related, water can destroy thing with minutes because of the force and weight content.

Now on the other hand, a hurricane like Katrina lasted for weeks, Katrina devastated the Florida coast line on August 25, 2005 then days later she devastated Louisiana, Mississippi, and Alabama on August 29, 2005 then several weeks later she came to a complete final stop alone the coast lines of the eastern great lakes on September 31, 2005, Hurricane Katrina was a rare phenomenon, and full of surprises.

The Katrina survivors struggled through the combination of various natural and man made disasters that history ever seen or hear of in America, many of the Katrina survivors waited over 6 days of suffering to be rescued.

The survivor were then displace into 44 states throughout America and then many were left homeless to flourish for themselves, some were able to come and some were not, they were push aside like yesterdays trash.

Months later various survivors were becoming suicidal they were not afraid of dying, they were afraid of what does it take to stay alive and start all over again from the beginning, the causes and effects of loosing everything made them suicidal, & now all faith and hope is gone, will and these suicidal victims death certificates entitled them as Katrina related deaths.

The aftermaths of hurricane Katrina was totally misunderstood throughout the world. At the hesitant efforts of Fema to reply and react to this emergency.

Months, weeks and days after hurricane Rita and hurricane Katrina various parts of the city of New Orleans stood flooded for months, rescue teams and clean up crew lost count of the dead bodies that was trap in attics, trap under tons of debris, trap in trailer, trap in building, trap in vehicles and various other places, dead bodies were everywhere, it appeared like a science fiction grave yard, but it was a harsh reality to see.

Nearly 200,000 homes was effected with toxic mole spores, nearly 12 times above average which made it highly toxic, to inbreathe

Months after Katrina various vehicle shattered by the flood water was still left unattended, those vehicles were covered with mole spores and parts of the city appeared to be a junk yard, mole spores look dirty and smell nasty.

The dead bodies throughout, the dead animals and the toxic mole spores made various cities smell like a garbage dump and look like a ghost town.

Many homes, businesses and apartment complexes had to be decontaminated for germ and disease control they were face with intense outbreaks of mole mildew spores and various other poisons

A special outfit was required by law to work indoors which was a spore repellent suit, boots and head mask to protect the human body from germ poison.

Many survivors homes were completely destroyed they cannot come back, more than 50 percent of the city own there own homes and most of them now are homeless.
In New York Katrina survivors were put out the hotel rooms at 3:00 am because Fema stop payment on the rooms.

In New Orleans some areas stood flooded for more than 60 days which includes the historic CBD area, which was my neighborhood area.

Very little repairs have been done throughout the city due to setbacks of various circumstances beyond control

The national guards troops were called into New Orleans to control the crime condition, the city was extremely chaotic due to a lack of assistances given to the public.

For several months heavy fog was appearing throughout the city making it difficult to see at night.

Many lives, properties and futures were change for the good, the bad and the ugly after Katrina.

Many survivors were living outside of New Orleans but was able to feel the pains and sufferings of what was going on inside New Orleans the adversity was dynamic for everyone to experience.

The first Christmas after Katrina was very sad for New Orleans people to experience and except, while after parts of the country was having a good time at Christmas. After shaking my testimonies with the people of Pennsylvania I was then ask by many of them to write a book and tell the dynamic compelling details and the different styles of adversities the human beings of New Orleans had to put up with to survive and cope and live.

Months after the storm, due to the overwhelming deaths, destruction and chaoticness in New Orleans many people were entice to commit suicide to rid there problems, which increase the suicidal rate to over 30 percent, then the suicide victims were documented as a Katrina related death causality.

If the disasters in New Orleans was a movie it would win all awards for the most compelling presentations ever seen display in America.

In the beginning of Katrina traffic near the airport was at a complete stop, some people abandon there vehicles to escape the storm then walk to the airport to catch a flight out of town to break away from the consequences to come soon.

Many survivors throughout the city did not have food, water, medical supplies or communication to help them cope with their circumstances of health, they struggle to survive for a long time.

Inside the historic CBD area of New Orleans that section of town did not have working electricity, gas, running water or telephone service for over two years. This situation left many survivor who lived in that area were now homeless in misery of what happen yesterday.

8 months after Katrina and the flood of New Orleans most of the city was experiencing large outbreaks of highly infectious contaminant spores from various poison with mole and mildew inside the homes, those homes must be immediately decontaminated for germ and disease control, but the mole and mildew and toxics keep coming back due to the aftermath poison effects the flood water left behind.

Months later a few survivors went back to New Orleans to visit they said, the city look like an old friend that was in a car accident and was severely disfigured, you know who the old friend is, but you just don't recognize them anymore it's a big difference, their face has change

80 percent of disaster throughout America are flood related, before the devastation of the twin towers of 911, in 1889 Pennsylvania had the worst flood in America, the water levels were beyond 80 feet high due to Dome breaches that collapse, the flood of 1889 killed over 2000 people throughout the cities effected in Pennsylvania's south fork Dam in Johnstown.
During Katrina aftermath
In 2005 Louisiana, Mississippi and Alabama experience the latest greatest floods in America, Mississippi had 90 percent of water, New Orleans had 80 percent and Alabama came in third highest water levels.

New Orleans will never be the same as before Katrina and the man made disaster of the enormous levee breach for various reason.

Katrina destroyed most of the gasoline stations in New Orleans and the gas tank pumps are built above ground which caused massive gasoline leakages throughout the areas effected, because gasoline is known to float on top of water, the fires throughout the city were severe and large fires were breaking out everywhere which was a drastic scenario to witness and experience. The fire department could not keep up with the massive outbreak of fires because 80 percent of the city was under toxic water.

The citizen of New Orleans and various other parishes were expose to high levels of contaminated toxic water which contained various chemical such as benzene, hydrochloric acid, chlorine, various oils and so on, which made it nearly impossible for the survivors to escape the grip of death.

The various chemicals, oils and gasoline's had contaminated air flowing throughout the cities effected and surrounding areas, no one was safe from the consequences that was face to face with them.

Many survivors were trap and waited for days to be rescued in horrifying condition which also includes various poisonous creature inside the water, which are snakes, eels, crabs, alligators and various large fish, and so on.

Many survivors were eaten to death by the gumbo of complication inside the mysterious surprises of the flood water of New Orleans.

Hurricane Katrina unleashed a grab bag of deadly tricks inside the gumbo of catastrophics throughout Louisiana, Mississippi, Alabama and so on.

The catastrophic monsters that emerge was one big death trap gumbo that happen by surprise and shock the world.

Katrina and various floods was the most supreme extraordinary combination of horrific disasters the central gulf coast has ever experience.

Katrina was a history making cataclysmic object that push many survivors of the storm into insanity and deeper poverty, which can lead to death in time

In 2011 many parts of New Orleans appears like Katrina struck yesterday, the city is still in bad shape in various ways and thousands and thousands of people still remain displace they have called a new place home.

For years after Katrina only 17 percent of city buses were in service and 7 percent of the public schools there have reopened, Katrina left her foot prints of massive annihilation all over the city many people from New Orleans realize they cannot live there anymore for a multitude of various reasons.

The city once called the Big Easy is now appearing to be the city of Big Misery and progress is slow you make do with what you got, many people think living in New Orleans is like standing on a tight rope without a net of support.

Within 5 southeastern states, Katrina was responsible for the thousands of deaths. Some estimates have put the reconstruction price to rebuild New Orleans at over 200 billion dollars, also including other cities throughout Louisiana and the gulf south.

The three most deadliest floods in America
<u>Inside the deep South</u>

1. The first most deadliest flood in America was in New Orleans in 1927, that flood killed approximately one million people and injured over several hundred thousands which then they were in need of food, water and medical attention, this disaster was cause by severe levee collapse.

2. The second most deadliest flood was in New Orleans in 1965, that flood killed over one thousand people and injured over several thousands, this disaster was cause by weather catastrophic hurricane Betsy, the storm over top the canal throughout the city.

3. The third most deadliest flood was in New Orleans in 2005, that flood killed over three to four thousand people and injured nearly eight thousand and effected over 100 thousand, this disaster was cause by levee collapse due to weather catastrophic of hurricane Katrina storm surge.

The combination of the three floods, which are 1927, 1965 and 2005 those floods killed one million five thousand, and injured and effected over five hundred thousand in less than a 80 year period, the three flood trio combined was the most extraordinary group of cataclysmic and catastrophic floods in the history of humankind. 80 percent of disasters throughout America are flood related.

But for several months after Katrina all public transportation was out of service

Throughout New Orleans and surroundings most supermarkets was damage and closed down, people drove to other cities to get food and other necessities of indispensable things to survive.

December 2005 in New Orleans and surroundings was the first Christmas season after Katrina which was a broken hearted season that brought psychological discomfort to them, it was a post matic stress time for my family and others

On December 15, 2005 was my mothers funeral, my mother Mrs. Dorothy Jacques died at the age of 87 years old, she drowned in the flood water at a nursing home for the elderly, her death is documented as Katrina causality related, she will be miss in our hearts and minds forever.

My Mother's Death

August 29, 2005, My beautiful and wonderful mother died in the water of the levee breach due to hurricane Katrina related death at the age of 87 years old, she is the mother of 10 grown children, she is also the mother of the author of this book Alvin Jacques.

This is what happen, at a local nursing home in New Orleans for the elderly, the nursing home director and staff members called the bus dispatch center several times by telephone for the rescue buses to hurry to the nursing home to quickly pick up the elderly to escort them to safe higher ground,

But the entire city was in great panic due to the coming of Katrina, the staff members at the nursing home had make a life on death decision for themselves, if to leave the building or if to stay in the building with the patients of elderly people, and time was running out.

Minutes later, the entire staff abandon the building leaving the elderly patients unsupervised and unattended to be face with the most deadliest natural disaster of consequences in America.

Moments later the levee breach flood crash into the nursing home building and killed every elderly patient in a flash, the flood water was 18 feet high of enormous strength filled with hundreds of deadly toxic poisons which then put the city of New Orleans under 80 percent of polluted water after the flood.

My beautiful mother's body weight was at 125 pounds before the flood water appeared, then later the deterioration factors of harsh toxic poisons and oil elements inside the flood water cause her skin to be completely eaten off of her body by those mixtures of chemicals and oil,

In the process of the aftermath cause my mothers body to be decompose, only her bones and eye balls remain, which then her body weight was at 15 pounds

The aftermath of Katrina was a harsh reality for everyone, at city morgue my mothers remains was misidentified 4 times by experts, two days later a leading optical expert identified my mothers eye balls as Mrs Dorothy Jacques.

We then learned the eye balls and bones of human being will out last the other parts of the human body.

Then after we identified the body as her remains, it then was refrigerated for more than 3 months inside the refrigerated truck center. Until New Orleans cleans the debris Katrina left behind

My mother funeral was then set for December 15, 2005 which is 10 days before the first Christmas after Katrina.

15 days later on December 31, 2005 my sister Mrs Maryanna Newman died at the age of 60 years old of a massive heart attack, the pressure of stress and our mother's funeral killed her, she will be miss in our hears and minds

15 days later January 15, 2006 my brother in law Mr Henry Woodfork Sr. died at the age of 65 years old of a massive stroke, the pressures of stress killed him, he will be miss in our hears and minds.

Within 35 days we had three funerals in our family, Katrina change our lives in many ways.

Hurricane Katrina was an example to how weather can change the course of history

These are real life stories of how the citizens of New Orleans endure unexpected adversities at high levels of intensity.

Throughout the city 1700 trailers was demobilize

Most of the people that was killed by Katrina there body reaming was stored inside refrigerated trucks to freeze or preserve it.

The First unforgettable mentor
Alvin Jacques Sr.
The Baron

My father Alvin Jacques Sr. was known as the Baron of our family of 10 children and a wife, he showed his 10 children how to develop strong values in life, the baron was a power house of knowledge with strange faith in God. We were taught to respect life and learn what goes around comes around, nobody gets away with ugly things in life, God in heaven watches everything we do in life and God is the key to success, God wants us to do the right thing or it will come back to haunt us, later in life I watch my father Alvin Jacques Sr. pray everyday on his knees every morning before he went to work and every night before he went to bed, he show us how to respect God and authority of him being a roll model example of our household and life in general.

My father got the name the Baron because he had great common sense and loved his wife and children above himself, my father was a great example of leadership in his household, he rise his children to be roll model at what ever they choose to do in life, but do it to be the best.

After my father's death on Sept. 7, 1976, he was 62 years old, his family, friends and others realize he would have made a great president of the United States because of his values, momentum and love for his family, friends and others the way god intended life to be, to believe in god is the ultimate in common sense, we are children of god and we must respect our Father in heaven always.

Now my mother and father are together once again, inside the hands of God, Amen.

My Last unforgettable Mentor
Elizabeth Angelety

My mother and father Dorothy and Alvin Sr. showed me the A, B, C;s of things, then my last mentor Elizabeth Angelety came alone and show me the XYZ's of things to make me a complete package.

Elizabeth Angelety promoted the idea to write my book, she was able to tell me what god was thinking of me and the potentials of the book, she was like a mother to me and could see into the future of my life, it was her gift from god, to see the future one her love one's, she was an extraordinary women & mother of 16 children I know it sound hard to believe a person could have such a gift as to see into the future, but Elizabeth Angelety was capable of doing it, I've travel around the world and have never encounter any one like her, when I said she was capable of telling me the XYZ of things it means she could tell me today what will happen tomorrow and blow me away, what ever she told me it happen in reality, Elizabeth Angelety was a Prophetess, a very good teacher, with the recipe of love in her heart, and soul.

Unfortunately on September 11, 2009 My auntie Elizabeth Angelety pass away at the age of 78 of cancer.

September the 11th is a monumental day in America it's the date of the death by destruction of the twin tower of 911 in New York.

Elizabeth Angelety left 10 grown children behind, she will always be remembered by many people as being a gift from God.

After Katrina deliberate arsons were out of control it was acts of maliciously setting fire to property and also due to busted gas pipes from the homes that were damage in the aftermath the fire was a hell inferno throughout the city as the fire burned day and night.

Mysterious killings were happening in the New Orleans area 6 people were found shot in the head inside there private home, killer unknown

8 people were found dead lock inside the bedroom closet, killer unknown

In another part of town 4 children and mother was shot and killed by grandparents.

Many people were suffering with psychological discomfort due to the problems of intense adversity surroundings.

The suicide rate was increasing daily as time pass on, it was the extraordinary time living in New Orleans for years after the after math of what Katrina left behind.

My private home in New Orleans was severely flooded but it was still standing in need of repairs, then out of the blue an arsonist maliciously lit my home a fire an it burned to ashes, alone with two other homes in the neighborhood which means there houses were burning at the same time, it was a triple play arson game.

I couldn't believe it really happen, but it was true, my home in New Orleans was completely gone, I was in Philadelphia at the time of the fire.

Then I called New Orleans demolition service to bulldoze the area and take the remaining of my home away, Now my property is just a vacant lot, all my memories of that house is gone, because of a crazy arsonist out of control.

The city of New Orleans had rodent rats over populating the city and levee borders

Rodent rats are capable of eating through all types of substances, the large Rodent rats can grow as big as the size of a regular cat and can weigh between 10 to 20 pounds.

The tail of a rodent rat act as a sensor element to navigate direction, and detect surrounding inside the underground sewer 80 percent of sewage waste is eaten by Rats, they do have an important role to play on earth.

The sewers is the headquarters residence were they live, play, multiple and grow, pumping stations and drainage pumps also serve as a active play ground nest for rodent rats.

A rodent rat can run quicker and faster than a cat or dog.

Streets of Blood

Many residence were not able to return to New Orleans, because of the various severe damages throughout the city.

Various cops beating the living hell out of various citizen throughout the city for fun and games because the could do it, they had the power. Cops were also shooting and killing people for no reason.

3 years after Katrina parts of New Orleans appeared as a large ghost town and smelled like a garbage dump, because the recovery may take years.

Nationwide armed gangs were ruling the streets of New Orleans, they were coming into the city by the thousands, Like rabbit dogs running wild.

Drive bye shooting was everywhere, the killer gangs just wanted to see fear, death and blood in the streets, But many of the drive bye killers were never caught for the crimes they committed.

Residence in New Orleans were isolated indoors they were paronoid, because of the crimes, killings and shooting throughout the city, everyone was in fear of their lives.

It's hard for the cops to be in shit all day and come home clean, Many of them forgot what the truth was,

Various cops were being set up by the feds because they were corrupt and greedy for blood money, Cops were killing cops for the love of money, Cops were lying about the killing because there was no witnesses to testify.

Most of the drug bus was divided among the cops, Cops were killing the dealers and gang members, Like they were the Pesticide and the dealers and gangs were the insects, for the love of money.

Various Lawyers were working alone with the cops to support the raid bus without a warrant, it was a case of one hand wash the other to get the money.

Various Prostitutes were killed and their tongues were cut out of their mouths, so they couldn't tell the cops were unlawful and dirty.

Many Cops were losing their tempers with each other, because the heat was on and time was running out, they were about to get eaten alive for the bullshit they committed time after time.

THE Mexican dealers was selling the drugs for the cops and the DEA, the mexicans would stop at nothing, they were stone crazy for drugs and blood money.

Everyone knows the huge disaster in New Orleans was basically more of a man made catastrophe. New Orleans experience over 42 billion in damages and Mardi Gras season 2011 was one of the biggest in 25 years, and tourist are slowly coming back.

But nearly 100,000 homes are still abandon with 90 percent of the historic CBD Ninth ward area still untouch and abandon. The overall recovery rate in New Orleans is slower then slow, and a large percentage of the population is on various pain killer or dope to cope.

The National guards and the police department patrol the streets of New Orleans day and night looking for trouble, Why do the police and other forms of justice kill people who kill people just to say killing is wrong, Could it be the turning point of justice, and the violence in New Orleans is in full swing as the shootings in the French Quarters get nationwide attention. And the crime rate in New Orleans is said to be five times more plentiful then anywhere else near bye.

If your traveling throughout New Orleans bring some serious protection or stay behind close doors from the element of surprise.

Many people throughout the city believe, the theory and methods of old New Orleans is out of position specially with the complexity of teenage thinking, New Orleans is like a foreign place with a different face under new management.

Life is full of various mysteries and surprises, And never underestimate the power of a catastrophe, And no one knows there destiny.

After Katrina many people had various properties filled with content that was uninsured and will never get paid for their loses.

Inside the superdome the survivors was a combination of poor, Middle class and high class people, which means sometimes no one is exempt from the grip of a disaster.

One thing for sure is displacement can rock your world, the aftermath of Katrina was a one of a kind, and the memories of that disaster will never die throughout the world.

It's base upon my faith I'm still alive today.

Many people will never overcome the aftermath complexities of hurricane Katrina and hurricane Rita, which both devastated the gulf coast only several days apart from each other.

Katrina help the man made levee breach to flood New Orleans with 80 percent of water, Then Rita increase the flood level height by several feet days later, And still waters run deep.

Days later after hurricane Rita various tornados and heavy rains touchdown on various cities, and started more devastation and displacements throughout the gulf, Then many people were very lost inside the massive series of horrific problems occurring, then Fema became more dysfunctional and disorganize with the multitude of intensities beyond their control.

Other countries from around the world offered to help America, But America thought they had things under control, But mean while various survivors were drowning and displacement reach an all time record high throughout 44 states.

Katrina, Rita and the manmade disasters was a demonstration of the various deception in our world we live in.

For day, weeks, months and years later after all was said and done, the people of New Orleans didn't know what it was like to be poorer then poor and be frustrated beyond reason, which usually creates fear and fear can create anger and anger has created the catastrophic crime scene in New Orleans.

The people are still face to face with problems of yesterdays aftermaths, and had to start their lives all over again, And some bad memories various people cannot overcome or escape it's a psychological discomfort to live with on a daily basis.

The hurricane Katrina survivors have served the purpose as role models and pioneers because what we endured was definitely legendary.

Streets of blood

The people in New Orleans had no other place to go as the mysteries unfold before there eyes, no body is safe in New Orleans

The police wanted to take back the city, but crime expert know, if the police take back the city it's a death sentence on the way.

On august 31, 2005 the mayor of New Orleans declare Martial law because a policeman was killed by a gun shot into the head, the order was do what you get to do, but later the mayor denied all allegations implications.

Month later at the Danzinger bridge in New Orleans 6 policemen open fire and shot 6 New Orleans citizens in need of food and medical attention, two of the victims died, the other four victims was severely injured, one of the four victims injured was shot 6 times

Then several months later the six police officers in the Danzinger bridge shooting face criminal indictments for there erratic menace behaviors.

These are real life true stores of the unexpected adversity due to the aftermath of Katrina that change the thinking of the people of the city

The people of New Orleans fear the police department more than the criminals, because the aftermath of Katrina the courts are gone, and the jails are gone, which means the police department had the freedom to do what ever they wanted to do at any time, and now the police was now above the law.

The term a ham sandwich is a gun that some unrighteous police have plant on innocent people to make them appear guilty of false charges.

For years dead body murders was being found in remote isolated places distantly related to the crimes in the city.

The power of a gun is incredible, the tommy gun was made in 1921 it shoots 600 times per minute, it one of first cruel machine guns to be made.

The police department in 2007 was a raging storm cops were killing the citizens, they eat the dead for pleasure

Undercover detectives were hassling people in the French quarters for pass time fun the French quarters was s death trap in action for the citizens and tourist, no body is safe in New Orleans. It's a psychological mess and a set back.

Innocent women were put in jail because they wouldn't surrender sexual favors & blacks were framing other blacks for false crimes throughout the city, it's a case of high deception.
Throughout the city gift shops were wipe out completely by armed gang members that was ruling the streets of New Orleans.

Many people were dealing drugs and the drive bye shootings throughout the city increase dramatically in some parts of town it was a war zone in action

Several months later Car thieves and drive bye shootings were out of control and murders were increasing people were killing people, due to the pains of adversity which was beyond control it was another world for New Orleans to experience. It's a struggle to survive and cope.

In 2007 and 2008 some of the biggest drug dealers and gangs moved to New Orleans, from other cities because New Orleans was open territory for the taking, Gangs and drug dealers were taking over as the drug power increase.

It was a new ball game now, Gang members from the other cities were killing the New Orleans citizens as a pass time thing nobody is safe anymore in New Orleans, it's a case of do or die.

Police in New Orleans are getting killed by those gang members and those gang members are getting killed by the outrage of the police department and the city is no longer the Big Easy.

The gang members and drug dealers were all about money and power and control over the city.

The police are corrupt in New Orleans, the police were raiding homes and trailer parks in search for the drug dealings to pocket the dope money, innocent people were killed in the process of these unlawful ideas put into action.

The greed for dope money was outstanding police are killing other police to get to the money first.

The feds are having shoot outs with policemen for control of the drug money it was chaotic

Then FBI agents were arresting the police for crimes of being dirty cops

The big time dope money and crimes in New Orleans had FBI, DEA, CIA and city cops recognize as dirty

Prostitution, pimping, drug dealing, drug addictions and crimes of various natures was in full swing in New Orleans for the love of money, they needed twice the sex but half the fourplay. The city is now a big masquerade

Music and entertainment is all night long in the city of New Orleans and surroundings, the night club scene close down between 4 am and 6 am in the early morning.

Alcohol of any types is sold 24 hours a day 7 days a week, alcohol can be purchase just about anywhere in the city which includes all supermarkets and grocery stores, shopping malls, convenient outlets, pharmacies, gas stations, restaurants, sandwich shops, night club and day time corner bars.

The alcohol consumption adds to the problems of drunk driving, violence, murders, and various other crimes, which happens throughout New Orleans and area surroundings

Inside the New Orleans French quarters a gay man got into a fight with his lover and was shot 22 times due to alcohol consumption and a violent temper.

In Meterie Louisiana 5 teenagers was shot 3 times each by drunken drive bye shooters, 2 of the teenagers died instantly the other were hospitalize

In Kenner Louisiana a drunk driver killed 6 people when he crash into a house at 4 am in the morning.

In the canal street area drunk drivers crash at 3:00 am into department store building but no one was hurt.

Inside the New Orleans French quarters sex and crimes is everywhere due to alcohol consumption and drugs and a love for money.

From February 20 to April 20, 47 murders happen inside the New Orleans area, in 2007 New Orleans has the highest murder rate and incarceration rate in America, also the highest poverty rate per capita.

The Ligo observatory sits 50 miles outside New Orleans which is a building for astronomical knowledge or other observations of weather activity.

Severe

On August 29, 2005 Katrina destroyed 4 large toxic chemical waste sights, the destruction of them release hundreds of various chemicals into the flood water.

At one of the toxic chemical waste sight more than 500 hundred chemical was discovered to be inside the flood water.

On the other side of town several oil refineries was destroyed they to release 7 million gallons of various oils into the water.

Altogether both chemicals and oils was escaping into the flood water entering into the city with enormous force which was creating a combination of chemical oil fusion which is a deadly compound it was keeping the water polluted to promote sickness then death

Various chemical of lead, benzene, arsenic and pesticide DDT have been accumulating at the bottom of the river and lake for years

Katrina whip them up from the bottom and sent them to the top which was inside the flood water that poured into the streets of new Orleans

Inside the whip up process mud was inside the flood water, the amount of mud was enormous it was enough mud to fill 300 thousand dump trucks the mud also had traces of poisons from years ago.

The chemicals, oils and poisons will remain airborne for many years which was confirmed by specialist of environmental control.

The 22 pumping station and 148 drainage pumps are connected the Lake Ponchatrain when the city pump the water out of the city, it was put back into the Lake Ponchatrain which is the drinking water supply for the city but very few know of that policy.

Specialist are not sure what the long term health impact will be for the future of New Orleans

The flood water created a mole epidemic in New Orleans, 200 thousand homes was effected but 50 thousand home are condemn to be destroyed because of super extreme levels of mole spores

To repair your home you must have less then 50 thousand cubic meters of mole spores is the limit

New Orleans had 12 times above the limit which was 600 cubic meter of mole spores

Most of the 30 thousand homes to be condemn are still standing 5 year later in 2010

Mole spore have health risk of sinus problem, lung infection, liver damage, pneumonia and brain damage

Environmental specialist predict the various contaminants, and health impacts could stay airborne for over 20 years which will impact the future of New Orleans and surroundings

The mole spore outbreak is just the beginning of the worse ecological disaster in America that Katrina and the levee breach flood left behind.

The combination of indoor mole spores with outdoor toxic airborne chemicals poisonings is an on going ominous life threatening risk to the people of New Orleans.

The mole spores keep coming back over and over it's nearly impossible to eliminate the spores completely

The boil water order 2010
In New Orleans

Five years after hurricane Katrina a boil water order was in effect on December 21, 2010 due to the poisons and pollution inside the city drinking water supply in New Orleans.

The citizens of New Orleans must boil there drinking water supply to drink and brush there teeth and limit there bathing time, the water is saturated with toxic chemical that won't go away, most toxic chemical reproduce themselves

The 4 toxic chemical waste sights Katrina destroyed 500 types of chemicals and oils was found inside the water, oil and poison mix together can preserve poison pollution to stay around, it's a fact of chemistry it's like glue.

Poisons have various side effects, which is common sense to believe, the ecological mayhem of the gulf oil spill could be increasing the intensity of the pollution of the water.

Due to the boil water order many people in New Orleans are concern what will the long term health impact will be for the future of the city.

P

You may have seen the recent news reports regarding potentially toxic Chinese drywall

Drywall is the board used to make interior walls, the defective drywall arrived at nearly two dozen ports around the country, these ports were in New Orleans, Florida, Texas, New York, and California

Usually drywall comes from within the United States, however due to a shortage during the construction boom along the gulf coast in 2004 and 2005 many builders imported drywall from China

Krauf Plaster board Tianjin Co. LtD of China, a subsidiary of German based manufacture Knauf, manufactured the drywall

P

This drywall was used in the United States after 2001. This drywall emit several sulfide gases into the home, which creates "a rotten egg-like" odor, the gases cause the accelerated corrosion of the air conditions and refrigerator coils, kitchen appliances and utensils, electrical wiring electronic or computer devices, and other metal surface and household items.

Long term exposure to low-levels of sulfides has also been associated with several health conditions including fatigue, loss of appetite, headaches, irritability, poor memory, dizziness, reproductive issues, apnea a sudden shortness of breath, irritated eyes, respiratory system irritation insomnia, and nose bleeds.

P

These symptoms will not go away until the drywall is removed from the home, or until you permanently leave the home.

How do you know if your home contains this drywall

1. The house has to been built or remodeled after 2001.

2. There may be and odor in your home that smells like one of the following rotten eggs, the smell of a match that has been struck and blown out, or a bit like fireworks.

3. you may have experienced repeated or continuous failure of your air conditioning coils or HVAC units or refrigerator coils

4. You may have experienced repeated or continuous failures of your kitchen house hold appliances, electronics, or computer devices

5. You may have seen corroded, or black electrical wiring in their walls in properties built, or remodeled since 2001.

6. You may notice that silver jewelry or silver plated utensils may be tarnished.

You can read more information on the toxic Chinese drywall on the internet by visiting homeowners consumers center.com

The authority

The word authority means to be a writer, everything on earth needs to have a blue print of understand to pass on to others to understand, authority comes from humility it helps others to comprehend meaning with words to describe the formation details and information to shape and form the results.

God is the superior and supreme authority and he gave us the letter of information which is called the bible, the bible was written in words of reality base on inspiration from god, the bible was compose to describe various consequences, circumstances, complications and considerations of the good, the bad and the most ugly in which the people on earth are face to face with day by day, God show us the results of life as we live it, and show us the aftermath of life between heaven and hell through the bible.

Faith is how we behave and act under trial
take the hurt and turn it over to god
we can learn from the ways of god
we can do all things through god who strengthens us.
If your faith is strong you will show it,
God will grow it, and others will know it.

All the catastrophic in the world put together equals one big force of catastrophic fusion that god is in control of at all times

It's not what happens to us that matters
It's how we react and feel about what happens to us that maters. It's all in how you think of it, you can become negative or positive the decision is yours

If you think differently, you can live differently it's a case of learning how to make something sweet out of the sour, it's called to prevail mind over matter.

The truth is you haven't lost everything if you still have a grip on your mind, it's called the power of reasoning.

Our dreams comes from god so does the help we need to achieve them, your money is not in your pocket, your money comes through your achievements of your mentality

God gave me many things to be thankful for but he didn't give me everything my way God has a different way of thinking compared to human beings, he knows the answers before we develop the thought

Jack the riper was violent because his mother abuse him for years he was lost in reality, Jack the riper killed his victims with a very shape knife, after he killed his victims he then took the kidney from out of there bodies, because he was angry at his mother and took his pain out on others.

After hurricane Katrina killings in New Orleans sky rocketed, most of the killers appeared to be charming but would kill with severe rage because their lives were shattered by hurricane Katrina and hurricane Rita, many of the killers lost everything and had to kill and steal to survive, many people went crazy because of those disasters, a catastrophic disaster can drive people insane because all hope and love is lost, and time was running out, like in Jack the riper.

After hurricane Katrina New Orleans is known to have some of the best criminal minds in the world because many people are killed on a daily basis, for entertainment.

The French quarter of New Orleans is the headquarters for the muggers and the gangs, but crime is everywhere throughout New Orleans everyday someone is severely injured or killed, the new Orleans incarceration rate is the highest in the Nation, but only have less then a population of a half million people.

Many people have loss sight and insight of the world we live in due to various catastrophics and economics, status quo from media is designed to keep you from dreaming and development, beware of status quo it can change your thinking and hold you in a box inside your own mind.

The Katrina survivors were seduce by status quo it change the good ones into the bad and then they became the ugly ones.

I'm the author of this book and formally a Katrina survivor, to write and finish this book about hurricane Katrina's aftermaths and others, I was put outside my comfort zone to do it, but I wanted the world to know my experiences and knowledge of the truth, Katrina effected my family, my friends and millions of others, everyone was face to face with the most unique extraordinary and uncompromising natural and man made supreme catastrophic disasters in American which also includes Florida, Mississippi and Alabama plus many others, remember the dynamics of those disasters around the world.

By being a Katrina survivor from inside the epicenter, I know what others are feeling from various set backs and disappointments from outside their comfort zone, I learn to be a big brother to many people and stay focus to finish my purpose on earth, sometimes various people around the world may not realize we are one big nation of human being under the will of god

My book is a catastrophic helper, it was design to help the now generation and the next generation to develop a better understand because of the various testimonies of the various wrath's of god.

A catastrophic disaster can take away everything material you own, but don't let it take your state of mind your mentality is your greatest investment stay focus.

From the day we were born our minds had a vision to do something and exceed outside our comfort zone it called the test of time to prevail, keep the faith.

Hurricane Katrina was a dynamic revelation, she was full force apocalyptic and the most extraordinary natural weather catastrophic catastrophe in the history of American throughout the South.

The most devastating causes and effects of hurricane Katrina was the elements of the aftermath surprises, from start to finish and the pass is the key to the present.

After all is said and done the only thing that matters is what we do for god. And a lack of forgiveness can create more problems for the future of humankind.

Forgiveness is the beginning of the healing process. Hold on and make the best of the ride.

Since Katrina New Orleans
Is not the same city

The New Orleans population has enormously decrease since Katrina, Orleans parish lost 29 percent of it's native residents, the surrounding city of St. Bernard parish lost nearly 50 percent of it's people as well.

The 2010 census report found that New Orleans population is now at 343,829 people in the city. The census report shows a population decrease of about 30 percent, that decrease means a less in political clout and federal dollars.

New Orleans is now a smaller city it loss over 118,000 African America with over 24,000 fewer whites Americans, New Orleans now have 33,000 more Hispanics and 3,000 more Asian the city is more international then ever.

Housing have increase in the suburb parishes and have very much decrease in the most heavily flooded parishes since Katrina. But in various areas of the city rent have nearly triple in price, generally speaking you pay more for less since Katrina.

Children under 18 years of various races are most unlikely to return back to New Orleans to live, in which they represent about 23 percent of the total population of the city.

Once every 10 years a census count is conducted by the United States census Bureau, which the New Orleans census provide critical knowledge about massive displacement caused by hurricane Katrina and the aftermath consequences throughout the city and surroundings, the total of displace citizens stands at over 200,000 people from New Orleans and surrounding.

Since hurricane Katrina of 2005 New Orleans lost over 140,000, since 1960 New Orleans lost over 288,000 people the city is smaller and different.

The Census report indicated the African Americans were first less likely to return back to New Orleans due to the circumstances after hurricane Katrina, the asian races was reported to be the most likely to return back to New Orleans for various reasons.

At this time as of 2010 the census indicated 118,000 few afro Americans live in New Orleans, 24,000 few white Americans live in New Orleans, 3,000 fewer Hispanics live in New Orleans, and 1,000 few Asians live in New Orleans,

The census report says after hurricane Katrina 189,000 homes were damage, effected by mole spores and was boarded up and classified as uninhabitable

Out of the 189,000 homes effected by Katrina and the massive flood 142,000 are now occupied and habitable which still leaves 47,000 homes germ effected, boarded up and classified as uninhabitable as of 2010 which is 5 years after Katrina the number of occupied and habitable homes have decrease by 24 percent.

The population in new Orleans as of year 2010 is 40 years behind time it's much the same as of year 1970, in the last ten years New Orleans lost nearly 66 percent of it's home town population.

The people of New Orleans are no strangers to adversity, in time their voices shall be heard.

Hurricane Katrina remains the most expensive natural disaster in American history, the aftermath effects of that storm displace over 200,000 people into 44 states of various location throughout American

The population of New Orleans has been diluted the decrease of native citizens was catastrophic it was similar to Humpty Dumpty that had a great fall, all the kings horses and all the kings men couldn't put humpty dumpty back together again, only the king himself is capable of putting humpty dumpty back together again. The Katrina survivors were called refugee's throughout America but those people were born in New Orleans and lived there for most of their lives.

The Ninth ward session of New Orleans was the epicenter which was the most destroyed area of the city were over 60 percent of the African American once lived, now the ninth ward area suffers greatly from neglect to be rebuilt, it has the slowest recovery rate throughout New Orleans, only 10 percent has been rebuilt since Katrina as of 2011.

The Limitations
Of Money

Written in simplicity of expression with a depth of thought

1. Money can buy you a book, but not a brain

2. Money can buy the medicine, but not the healing

3. Money can buy a companion, but not a true friend

4. money can buy influence, but not salvation

5. Money can buy sex, but not real love

6. Money can buy pleasure, but not the purpose

7. Money can buy entertainment, but not valuable happiness

8. Money can buy a expensive bed, but not a goodnight sleep

9. Money can buy power, but not wisdom or understanding

10. Money can buy the world, but cannot buy your soul

Your talent is a gift from god, it what you do with that talent is your gift to god.

Alternatives to become Stronger

1. Have the heart of a lion,

2. The force of a tiger,

3. The strength of a elephant,

4. The lives of a cat,

5. The patients of a donkey,

6. The moves of a monkey,

7. The balance of a crane,

8. The vision of a eagle,

9. The stillness of a owl,

10. The nose of a wolf,

11. The grip of a Gorilla,

12. The back bone of a horse,

13. The boldness of a panther,

14. The bit of a crocodile,

15. The speed of a fly,

16. The sting of a snake,

The Eagle and the Chicken
A True Story

Eagel's don't flap there wings in the barn yard like the chicken does, Eagels soar with grace through the sky with the power of the wind beneath their wings.

Eagel's are very focus they can see for miles and miles, they have tunnel vision in their scope, and can see a storm before it comes, Eagel's are not afraid of storms, they enjoy new adventures, they are curious, brave and bold.

In fact the eagel prefers to have fun in high wind storms so the wind currents can push them higher above the storm and clouds to reach altitudes of new levels.

The eagel have the personality and the courage to be the most daring creature in the sky. they are the leaders of innovation, and watchfulness.

Eagel's are fearlessly committed to get what they set out to get, they stay focus on something and do not get distracted, they get the job done.

In fact the airplane was built and designed from the diversities on an eagel, which is to soar through the sky in various ways to reach it's destination target plan.

Chicken's don't soar through the sky, Chicken like to flap their wings standing on the ground, while the eagle flies above the clouds at no price to demonstrate their god given ability to learn new discoveries.

THE bible says they that wait on the Lord to deliver them will mount up with the wings and the vision of an eagle, the eagel knows it got what it take to experience the unknown discoveries, of new adventure into the beyond, and Eagel don't go running around flapping their wings like chickens in the barn yard wishing they could fly.

The Gulf Oil Spill

On April 20, 2010 50 miles off the coast lines of Louisiana a huge oil rig burst unto flames and dynamic explosions, THE Vessel had 126 men aboard, THE heat of the fire was able to reach a half mile away, And then things got worse, THE fire was so intense other emergency crews were brought in from holland and texas to help with the out of control oil spill disaster of fire and flames.

11 men were missing in action as the fire and explosions increase rapidly, parts of the huge oil rig collapse, the large crane aboard the vessel melted from fire, the underwater rig cables are 5 thousand feet below the water, the cable broke apart from the main connection it created more oil to excape to add to the consequences.

Moments later the coast guards were on the scene there mission goal is to save lives, THE massive flames of fire was at 200 feet high, Oil can burn more intensely then gasoline and the source of the fire is crude oil in large amounts.

The next April 21, 2010 at 10:22 AM the entire huge oil vessel sank to the bottom of the gulf, the crude oil hole was approximately one mile long, it release thousands of gallons of oil daily.

Then the oil spread towards an east-westward direction then thousands of gallons of oil was appearing on top the water, Many worldwide experts believe 200 thousand gallons is coming out daily, but that's four time more ten we are being told by the media.

British Petroleum BP is responsible for the ecological occurances, 40 percent of BP is owned by american share holders, the oil spill is viewed through worldwide eyes, as the problems increase for months.

The crude oil is now concentrated tar balls, it's like big balls of jelly, it's effected seafood and wildlife throughout Louisiana, the oil spill has also effected large boat yards in Grand Isles LA. and in New Orleans the oil is out of bounds.

Unfortunately the oil spill was left unattended for a while, it seems like the clean up crews were not doing a good job, And the oil is continuously escaping to be more plentiful.

Various underwater robots, Mud packs, Top Kills, Jake shots, and other methods were being used to stop the oil spill disaster but unfortunately nothing was working effectively.

Many businesses were dynamically effected by the set backs the oil spill created, such as the seafood industry, the hotel industry, the Restaurant industry, the tourism industry, And many others were feeling the pressure of the oil spill disaster, alone the gulf coast region, such as Florida, Mississippi, Alabama, Louisiana and many others the list go's on and on.

The enormity of this oil spill can travel to other places, and create other cases of misery And setbacks, And other various consequences.

There is absolutely no amount of money that can make up for the setbacks, damages, nightmares and heartaches this ecological monster has created.

Throughout various locations thousands and thousands of various subject have change for the worst such as various human Lives, various Businesses, various Livelihoods, various Marine Life, various Wildlife, And the beauty of various wetlands and other properties for a long time to come.

This was another story about the major endurance and psychological discomfort many people throughout the gulf experience, only several years after hurricane Katrina mesmerize them severely. But must I say that history has a reputation of repeating itself and does lighting strike twice in the same place.

However you think of it, the south region was and is face to face with another large portion of the Catastrophic Gumbo mixtures of disasters with them all taking place and being stir around at the same time.
Why do disasters happen

Within the last few years from 2004 thru 2011, Earthquakes, Tsunamis, Tornados, Hurricanes, Floods and various other natural & man made disaster are occurring throughout the world.

Disasters are becoming more abundant, more dynamic and more unpredictable, which means we are all subject to various trails, tribulations, persecution, pressures and enormous setbacks we may be unable to avoid.

Everyone needs love and peace and the Lord is coming soon, this is not a petty tail, Jesus is coming back, Except Jesus as your personal savior, the various disasters around the world is not a joke to laugh at, the element of surprize will catch anyone off guard, And wrap them up.

There is a price to pay for ignoring god, And god controls the element of surprize and the signs of the times, But many have turn there backs on god, It's time for us to keep our heads to the sky, we need to have our hearts ready.

God is Lord, and God still oversee everything that happens, with all the crimes, wars, deception and disasters it telling us that god has various judgements against the world.

If Adam and Eve would have never sin, we would not have chaos on earth today, Confusion is a sign of the devil, But can we loose our salvation, only if we refuse to love, believe and obey god, otherwise your name in heaven will be erace, Forever.

The question is who committed the first sin on earth, was it adam and eve or the serpent. The answer is the serpent was first to sin before adam and eve were born.

If your blind to the signs of the times, watch pray and live in faith, Jesus is the river of life, When everybody walk with Jesus, everyone will rise to the top and change the world.

Jesus is able to save us, believe in yourself. No pain, no gain means to endure through to shadows of time, be a witness and a light to others, And nothing is impossible with neighborly love.

The 2 most important commandments of the ten commandments are, to love god with all your heart and soul, And to love thy neighbor as thy self. Then the other 8 commandments will come auto matically.

Having respect for God and your neighbors will let nothing go undone, we will see things we never saw before, it could be the most wonderful time in history. Believe in yourselves.

It's time to love people through life, And man is the spirit of leadership and women should support his spirit for the good of all nations, Amen.

THE Various

Continent, Countries, States, Cities, population and Vehicles.

1. Throughout the world the 7 continents are listed by content size. they are

1. Asia - the biggest
2. Africa
3. North America
4. South America
5. Europe
6. Antartica
7. Australia - THE oldest

---

2. Throughout the world the Number of Various Countries are between 193-195 locations.

---

3. Throughout the world the number of various States equals 812 locations.

---

4. Throughout the world the number of various Cities are 1509 location, And 1054 of those cities have a population of more are less then 500,000 people, And 455 of those cities have a population of more or less then 1,000,000 people.

---

5. Earth has a population of 6.7 Billion people, And 20 percent of them are in need of food to eat.

6. The number of vehicles on earth is between 700 to 800 million which equal 10 people for every one vehicle on earth.

7. The Average numbers of houses-per-city block is between 5 to 10 and some neighborhoods may VARY.

Knowledgeable Tips about New Orleans

1. THE Music of New Orleans contain a wide variety of Cajun, African, Cuban, Latin, Caribbean, Soul and American Blues all wrap up together like a gumbo, But American Blues represents a disaster, If it's not a disaster it's not the Blues.

2. New Orleans is the Gumbo Mixture recipe for Food, Music and cultural diversity.

3. New Orleans has the most Jazz Festivals and Food Festivals in the world, featuring Music and Food from around the world every year.

4. New Orleans is known around the World for some of the greatest, Trumpeters, Pianist and drummers on earth.

5. Three of the greatest Trumpeter from New Orleans are Louis Armstronge, Al Hirt and Wenton Marcellest.

6. Three of the greatest Pianist from New Orleans are Fat's Domino, Professor Longhair and Dr. John.

7. Three of the greatest Drummers from New Orleans are Smokey Johnson, Herman Ernest and Alvin JacQues Jr. which is the author of Catastrophic Gumbo Part I and II.

8. New Orleans has the biggest and most diverse Mardi Gras festivities in the world, that features some of the greatest Marching Bands and entertainment from around the World.

9. THE Phrase a second line originated from the grove and intensity of a Mardi Gras Parade in action, A second line means to let the good times role on and on.

10. New Orleans has one of the biggest ship docks in the world, that bring various people from around the world to visit.

11. Hurricane Katrina was the biggest Natural disaster in america that touch down on New Orleans in a monumental way and change the population, and the original momentum of various locations forever.

12. New Orleans is one of the biggest tourist attractions in the world, and the memories of hurricane Katrina still go's on and on.

Here's a list of various musical and outstanding families of excellent reputation to carry out the tradition in New Orleans.

The Batiste Family	The Perrault Family	The Morial Family
The Neville Family	The Francis Family	The Leon Family
The Joseph Family	The Woodfork Family	The Mercandell Family
The Domino Family	The Morrison Family	The Angelety Family
The Kerr Family	The Johnston Family	
The Marcellis Family	The Anderson Family	
The Jacques Family	The Newnan Family	
The Charbonnet Family	The Hutchson Family	

AND the list go's on and on.

Life is relative it's what you make of it that counts Throughout my time on earth, I learned there is value and promise even in the toughest time. During hardships or heartacke, I become truly teachable, In the trasition from darkness to light, I gain new understanding about myself and about life, then I find the strenght and resilence to go straight ahead, and then I am ready to rise and see all the various things life has to offer.

While living in Pennsylvania I had a profile design of 38 years of my musical background and thankyou to everyone I've work with alone the way through the years.

Endorsement Credits & Special Thanks
JD Calato Regal Tip Sticks
Special thanks to: Carol Calato & Vonick
Vater Percussion
Special thanks to: Alan & Ron Vater
Pure Cussion
Special thanks to: Kent Peterson
Taye Drom Co. Orange County Cali
Special thanks: Taye Drum Co, Juan Labostrie

Alvin Jacques

Special Thanks
To The
Hyatt Regency, Double Tree,
Hotel Inter=Continental, Fairmount, Meridian,
Sheraton and Wyndham Hotels for giving me
the honor to provide the entertainment as an
Agent/Manager when I was unable to perform personally

Letters can be presented upon request

38 years of International Professionalism & Accomplishments Accomplished By:
Mr. Alvin Jacques
1970–2008

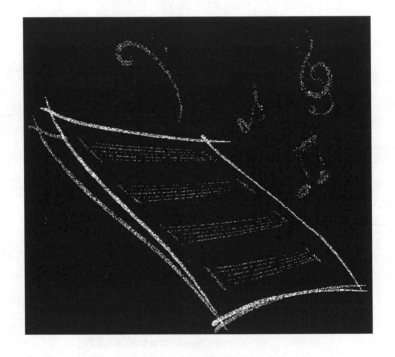

Featuring
The Alvin Jacques International Trio Plus

Also Featuring other
Accomplish Entertainers, Recording Artist
Sponsors and Industry Giants

Details inside

National & Int'L Conventions and Special Events featuring Alvin JacQues and the Alvin JacQues Int'L Trio Plus

1. Percussive Arts International -1992
2. Percussive Arts Society International Convention
3. Colgate- Palmolive Convention
4. Ford Motor Company (Private Dinner party)
5. Mitsubishi Motors (Private Dinner party)
6. American Automobile Association (Company party)
7. National Bar Association of Aviators Convention
8. A.C.A.A. Convention
9. N.A.D.A. Convention
10. National Association of Newspaper's Convention
11. TKS U.S.A., Inc Convention
12. Johnson & Johnson Services, Inc. Convention
13. Brand Scaffold Services, Inc. Convention
14. Southern Ass. of Dairy Food Manufacturers, Inc. Conv.
15. CBS (soundtrack, personal appearance in movie, rap up)
16. Panduit Corp. (Autograph session prior performance)
17. Ortho- clinical Diagnostic convention
18. Elected Officials for the Unite States Whitehouse Conv.
19. Louisiana State Supreme Court (Election Night)
20. Government & other officials of law and order (special event)
21. WUG- Uniworld Group Inc. Convention
22. Colgate-Palmolive Presidential luncheon
23. Arnaud's Restaurant (special event)
24. Travel Concepts, Ltd (special event)
25. Jazz Educators Society Int'l, Convention 2000
    (By Special Request of the Hyatt Regency New Orleans)

New Orleans Hotels
Letters of Support & Recommendation

1. Hyatt Regency - Hotel New Orleans
2. Double Tree - Hotel New Orleans
3. Hotel-Inter-Continental New Orleans
4. The Fairmount Hotel at University Place New Orleans
5. Le Meridian Hotel New Orleans
6. Sheraton Hotel New Orleans
7. Marriot Hotel New Orleans
8. Wyndham Hotel New Orleans
9. Prince Conti Hotel New Orleans
10. Maison Dupuy Hotel New Orleans
11. Holiday Inn Downtown Superdome New Orleans

Business Corporation

1. T.K.S. (USA), Inc.
2. National Association of Newspapers
3. Southern Association of Dairy Manuf. Inc
4. Brand Scaffold Service, Inc.
5. WUG- Colgate-Palmolive-Uni-world Group Inc.
6. J.D. Colato Regal tip Sticks
7. Vater Percussion
8. Pure Cussion-Shell Drums
9. USA Social Security Administration
10. Arnaud's Restaurant
11. Travel Concepts LTD

Everyone: Thanks You for your support

MR. ALVIN JACQUES
ENDORSEMENT & SPONSORS

1992 PASIC held at New Orleans Hyatt Regency

1992 The Alvin Jacques Trio performing live nightly at the New Orleans Hyatt Regency Hotel & Resorts. For the first time in New Orleans on November 11 - November 17, 1992, the trio entertained the Percussive Arts Society International Convention, one of the world's largest Musician's Conventions. The Alvin Jacques Trio entertained the world's most famous Drum Companies and more than 50,000 musicians. Sponsored by the New Orleans Hyatt Regency Resorts.

SPONSORED BY:
ENDORSEMENT CREDITS:

1992 **J.D. Calato Regal tip Sticks** • Niagara Falls, NY
Personalized Signature Series Drum Stick Endorsements 1992 thru 2001

1992 **Vater Percussion** • Holbrook, MA
Personalized Signature Series Mallets and Drumsticks
Endorsement: 1992 thru 2001

1992 **Percussion - Shell Drums** • Minneapolis, MN
Endorsement: Several sets of Shell Drum sets and accessories 1992 thru 1997

1992 **Evans Drum Heads and Accessories**
Endorsement: 1992 thru 1997

1993 **New Orleans Hyatt Regency Hotel**
Mr. Alvin Jacques is the first drummer and music artist in New Orleans to be honored with having his personal photograph and personalized signature series drumsticks framed at placed on the Wall of Famous Performers; located in the Hytops Lounge in the New Orleans Hyatt Regency Hotel.

October 24, 1999   **Ponduit Corp Trade Show** held at NOCC
Title: Signature session, Autograph Performance
Artist: Soloist Alvin Jacques
NOCC: New Orleans Convention Center
Panduit: Chicago, IL. Sponsored by Panduit, Debra Somlin and Wyndham Hotel

2001   **Award Credits** • Mr. Alvin Jacques, Drum Clinician
The United States of America
The Social Security Administration N.O. Bywater SSA Office
February 15, 2001 - Mr. Alvin Jacques was presented a plaque, round
trip female chauffeured, a letter of an accolades other emanates in
appreciation and recognition for an outstanding performance at
their (2nd) black history program. Sponsored by Brenda Douglas
Shepherd

2006 **Taye Co. Drum Endorsement**
The export coor pro drums with cymbals paste 2002
Sponsored by Taye Drum Co., Mr. Juan Labostrie and New Orleans

2006 **LF Drums Endorsement**
The Alpha Drum Set with Cymbals
Sponsored by Mrs. Darlene Hutchison (NO, LA)
Christine Hutchison

2007 **DDrum Endorsement**
Studio Drum set with Zildjian Cymbals
Sponsored by BL, PA

2007 **Wuhan Cymbal Endorsement**
Wuhan Hand made Cymbal & Gifts
Sponsored by Musicians Friend Inc.
Medford, Oregon

2008 **Mapex Drums Endorsement**
Stage Drums
Sponsored by Want & Co. PA

2008 **Workshop Inc** • New York, NY
Stage Apparels
Furnished by Workshop Inc., New York,

2008 **Pulse Professional Drum Endorsement**
Elite Series Drums & Cymbals
Sponsored by Musicians Friend Inc.
Medford, Oregon

TV, RADIO & NEWSPAPER

September 1995   **WGNO (Ch. 26)**
Filmed in New Orleans at the Home of Alvin Jacques a 30 minute interview about the art of the drum, reviewed on the air for 43 weeks
Sponsored by WGNO (Ch. 26) New Orleans

September 1996   **WWL (Ch.4)**
New Orleans Documentary
Special thanks for outstanding performance they attend and for the gift of a pair of his Signature Series Drum Sticks
Sponsored by Anchor Man Executive New Reporter, Eric Pulson & (Ch. 4) New Orleans

TV
Ch. 4, 6, 8, 26, 12, 38, in NO and abroad
Appeared also on CNN, World coverage, Live Interviews
Reviews appeared in Newspaper, Local and abroad for XXX years

1992 - 2005   **Newspaper**
Daily, weekly and monthly advertisement throughout New Orleans
Sponsored by clients of entertainment

1992 - 2005   **Live Radio**
WWOZ Radio 90:7 New Orleans
Live Interviews, Live Performances and Reviews
Sponsored by WWOZ Radio, New Orleans 90:7

2005 - 2006   **Televised in 2005**
CNN World News Report
Live Interview, Alvin Jacques in New Orleans
Sponsored by CNN

MR. ALVIN JACQUES
PROFESSIONAL RELEVANT STAGE EXPERIENCES & PERFORMERS

1970 - 1982 Reowned Int'l Entertainers & Recording Artists & Professionals
1970   The Platters
1972   The Club Med Band - Quartalope Caribbean
1973   The Chocolate Milk Band
1975   Professor Longhair
1978   Frankie Brent
1980   Tommy Ridgley and the Untouchable

1982 - 2005 Professional Relevant Stage and Studio Experiences
Reowned Int'l Entertainers & Recording Mists & Professionals

1982 - 2005 The Drummer with Various Stage and Studio Modern and Traditional Jazz and Groups include:
Thomas Jefferson, Milton Baptiste, Al Hurt, The Olympia Brass Band and the Rockets and others

Funk, Rhythm and Blues Bands include:
Fats Domino, Irma Thomas, The Dixie Cups, Dave Bartholomew, Lloyd Price, Earl King, Professor Longhair, Tommy Ridgley, Johnny Adams, Chocolate Milk, King Floyd, Wanda Rouzan, Charmaine Neville and Jean Knight and others

Pop Bands include:
Joe Simpson, Rickie Monie and Carol Merriweather and others

Jazz Latin Bands include:
Phase IV, Coco Samba, LLB Project and Cobra Plus Alpha 5 and others

DRUMMER IN MUSICAL AND STAGE PERFORMANCE
1992 "Lady Bug" Musical on the life of Billy Holiday, Emerson's Bar and Grill, starring Wanda Rousan, Lanie Robertson, Writer, Tommye Myrick, Director, Sam Henry, Music Director, Alvin Jacques Stage and Drums

THEATER PERFORMANCE
1970 - 1992 Locations: New Orleans, New York, the Caribbean

JAZZ & MUSIC FESTIVALS
1975 - 2005 Locations: New Orleans, Canada, the Caribbean, Europe, South America, etc.

GOVERNMENT PERFORMANCE
1970 - 1973 The American Embassy in South America and the Caribbean Islands
1971 - 1982 The USA Military Troop and officials in Europe the Caribbean and the USA
1993 The USA White House Convention, held at Double Tree Hotel, New Orleans
1994 The Louisiana State Supreme Court Convention, Fairmont Hotel New Orleans

The Musicians that Performed & Produced with
The Alvin Jacques Int'l Trio Plus in the New Orleans Hotel Industry

Bass	Piano	Hotel
Richard Payne	Bruce Ellison	Hyatt Regency Hotel
Charles Moore	Richard Kcox	LE Meridian Hotel
Herbert Wing	Sam Henry	Wyndham Hotel
Mark Brooks	Mari Watanabe	Fairmont Hotel
Jim Singleton	John Mahoney	Sheraton Hotel
Alton Herrin	Steve Berchawell	Double Tree Hotel

The Alvin Jacques Int'l trio Plus was formed in 1990
The Alvin Jacques Int'l Trio Plus was formed in 1990

PROFESSIONAL RELEVENT WORK EXPERIENCE
Actor, Studio Recording, Television

Actor on Talk Drums in CBS World Premier Movie in 1991
March & April 1991 CBS World Premier (Love & Curses)
Mr. Alvin Jacques was dressed as an African and played the African talk drum
Produced and directed by Gerald McRainey and Delta Burke
Filmed in New Orleans, LA

CBS World Premier Movie in 1991 Studio Sound Track
"Love and Curses" Filmed and recorded in New Orleans, with Gerald McRainey and Delta Burke, Directors and Milton J. Batiste, Jr., Musical director. Alvin Jacques accompanied 37 musicians in five separate bands and developed the full soundtrack for the movie. Recorded at Seasaint Studio NO, LA

1991 **Tommy Ridgley & Seasaint Studios**
Title: She turns me on and I love you
Artist: Tommy Ridgley

Dubat Music Publishing
Title: Embraceable Melodies
Artist: Al Carson & Milton Batiste

1992 **Mardi Gras Record Inc.,** World Premier
Title: Christmas in New Orleans
Artist: Charmine Neville, Tommy Ridgley and many more

1994 **Mardi Gras Recording Inc.**
Record in New Orleans World Premier
Title: Bourbon Street Jazz after Dark
Executive Producer: Warren Hillder Bran

April 1995 **Live at Le Meridien Hotel**
Produced by: WWOZ Radio World Premier
Title: Breeze Bop

February 1996 - November **Fairmont Hotel**
Recorded in New Orleans, LA Recorded Live
Title: Alvin Jacques Center Jazz
Executive Producer: Alvin Jacques

1999 Mardi Gras International Records, Inc.,
Recorded in New Orleans World Premier
Title: Mambo Number 5 Lou Bega
Executive Producers: Warren - Hillder Bran, Mardi Gras Record Inc.

Education Report
Elementary: Valenia C. Jones
Junior High: Epiphany
Senior High: St. Augustine
University: Dillard/Loyola

International Travel Report:

Mr. Alvin Jacques Professional career started at age sixteen in 1970. Mr. Jacques has gained International Experience Performance Experience and Stage recognition in Various Countries inside the Continent of South America Europe, Asia, Australia, The Caribbean and United States.

Mr. Alvin JacQues
International Travel Summary Report Include = Continents, Countries, Cities, and Occasions

South America

Venezuela - Caracas	Hotel-Inter-Continental
Brazil - Rio, St. Pablo	Hotel-Inter-Continental
Columbia - Bogota, Cali	Hotel-Inter-Continental
Peru - Lima	Hilton Hotel
Argentina - Buenos Aires	Hilton Hotel

Europe

Holland - Amsterdam	Concert Tour
Germany - Berlin	Concert Tour
Belgian - Brussels	Concert Tour
France - Paris	Concert Tour
Spain - Barcelona	Concert Tour

Asia & Others

Japan - Tokyo	Hotel-Inter-Continental
China - Bangkok	Hotel-Inter-Continental
Korea - Seoul	Hyatt Regency Resort
Canada - Quebec/Montreal	Jazz Festivals
Australia - Sydney	Sheraton Hotel

The Caribbean West

Haiti - Porta Prince	Hotel Dumbala
Dominican Republic - Santo Domingos	Hotel-Inter-Continental
Cuba - Guantanamo	Concert Military
Puerto-Rico - San Juan	Hilton & Holiday Inn Hotels
St. Lucia - Prasli Bay	The Buccaneer Hotel

The Caribbean East

Trinidad - Porta Spain	Hotel Hilton
Barbados - Bridge Town	Stadium Concert
St. Martin - St. Martin	Le St. Martin Hotel
Guadeloupe - Ave. / Europe	Club Mediterrain
Martinque - Ave. / Europe	Club Mediterrain

The United States

New York - Manhattan	Sheraton Towers
California - Beverly Hills	Hilton Hotel
Nevada - Las Vegas	MGM Hotel
Chicago - Illinois	Hyatt Regency Resort
Louisiana - New Orleans	Fairmont Hotel

Airlines and Ships Performance
KLM Airlines
Air France Airlines
Caribbean Cruise Lines
New Orleans Showboat Cruise Lines

Acknowledgment Report
Mr. Alvin JacQues has experienced other exotic cultures, lifestyle, concepts, music, rhythms, and colors that is still a treasure to him today

Alvin Jacques